For those in pain or being mistreated.

The Healing Diary

Healing Diaries Publishing
www.healingdiaries.com

Edited by Lynne Heinzmann

Cover artwork by Martin Cruz Venegas
Cover design by Jenna Grace Orsini
Cover concept by Yana Goncharov
Cover concept by Katherine Koehler

Author photo by Liana Kurguzov

THE HEALING DIARY

Friday October 20th 2017,

Was all of this worth it? And if it was, will I ever know? Will I die before the deepest questions in my soul are answered? This world feels like the description of hell sometimes. I am tortured now with a denying father and physical unrest. My mother's shocked by this situation, my sister's distant with me, and I can't imagine having a lesser opinion of my dad.

Why have You put so much before me?

The concept of "walking with God" crashes my intellect to a halt in moments of despair.

Every layer of me belongs to You. Why don't You just control me in all verbal, motor and spiritual ways? We would have an easier, more productive walk this way. It's difficult to trust the tugs of Your Holy Spirit/the fluttery feelings You put in my tummy.

Help me.

Saturday October 21st 2017,

Unfortunately, life sucks terribly. I feel… I feel like I am in the worst emotional and mental state of being you could ever be in. What am I supposed to do? I don't recognize myself in the mirror, and I don't want to. I'm ashamed of the way I look.

The pain in my body is kind of unreal… Why is there still so much pain because of what he did to me? And why am I feeling it now? After all these years? And what is this dramatic expectation of holding myself to the highest standard of knowing what to do?

Sunday October 22nd 2017,

I can't sleep. My mind's racing with the speed of the fastest car. This is a good ride though, there's clarity on the track. Yet, while the fuel of truth energizes me, my body is depleted. I do have some weed in the corner of my room… Hmm, it's already too late in the night. I wouldn't wake up in time for my day tomorrow

- Responsible
- Responsible

That's what I should be.

I am asking for and expecting Your clarity. Carry my mind to a place of receptivity.

Father, during quiet time with You, You've brought me a name to remember. It's the name of a man who knew about my father's abusive acts and didn't do anything about it. What am I to do now? In the stressed, raised eyebrow pocket it will go.

I trust You.

Tuesday October 24th 2017,

When I believe You enough to know You'll move mountains, I get to see You move them. I thank You that I have no fear of death. I sense huge plans for my future, and THANK GOODNESS because if they weren't big, I'd have a hard time finishing this journey with any sliver of gung-ho.

Wednesday October 25th 2017,

I looked up some descriptions of hell this morning. I'm not in it. I thought I was for a moment. Okay—not **really** but I wondered if maybe I was somewhere in between life and suffering the consequences of my sins. **Earth:** The never-ending loop of a sad foot race that can be convincing of the latter.

I spoke to the Clackamas County Detective about recent recalling's today. They seemed significant. He's easy to speak with. He knows pain.

Church Sins
A Poem by Shayla Danielle Laurendeau

I believe God wants to cause and show
His total and healing reconciliation, so
He uncovers the lies
in the Church.

If God was welcomed into more homes, more schools and more businesses, I believe we would see Him generously flipping every lie into the light. It'll happen anyways, so we might as well welcome Him to do it.

"For God will bring every work into judgment, including every secret thing, whether good or evil." – Ecclesiastes 12:14 NIV

The truth is: the **harder** I have fought to walk with God, the **trickier** satan's attempts have been in tripping me, BUT the goodness of my closeness with Yahweh is that it is **harder** to trick me. The more I learn about God, the more I am able to recognize the enemy's lies—i.e., the more I know of God's generous character the more I am able to identify what is deceitfully twisted.

What if the scoliosis in my spine is from him? He'd come up behind me in the middle of the night and I'd seize up… My whole spine would compress as I turned to stone…

Monday October 30th 2017,

My jaw is tight. I don't have a single human I can tell everything to. Droning surface conversations that are the normal of this world (and have little to do with the purpose of human existence) have been choking me slowly.

I don't know how to live right now. I have let only one friend know **some** of what I'm working on. That is: giving all of my moments over to peace, and a slower pace, for a better life.

```
Every  breath  I  breathe  reminds  me  of
gravity's heavy weight.
```

```
I'm sitting here engaging the back of my
throat [always] so my jaw heals. Praise
God for guiding me out of this pain.
```

Tuesday October 31st 2017,

I'm at Starbucks. It's 1:10PM and my insides have colored my outsides gray. I feel alone and like I'm floating (in a bad way). HOW LONG ARE LIE DETECTOR TESTS ANYWAYS? Why hasn't my phone gone off with a buzz from the detective? Did he lose my number? Did he get busy with other detective work? What if my dad is such a good liar that he passes the lie detector test with no sign that he's lying? He's practiced for years. He's practiced lying for my whole lifetime.

Anxiety is rushing through my body even though one of the nine browser tabs I have open is www.bible.com. I've already gone through three days' worth of devotions, and yet, my pulse's pace makes me feel like I am the one about to be checked for lies.

```
I cannot wrap my head around believing the
bible's promises of what is coming to
```

4

bless me. It's too much right now. Right
now, it's too good to feel real.

Last night was one long, bug-eyed wide-awake sad-song. I
begged the Most High to cause my father NOT take his life
because of his interview today with the Detectives.

WHAT THE: AHH.

It's evening now and my boyfriend asked me if I wanted to go
to a party tonight. How could I party tonight? I know he hears
the steady deadness in my voice.

I told him, "Do whatever."

Why didn't I tell him I'd rather have him by my side?

Chaos went down during the lie detector test earlier. They
ended up sending my dad away in an ambulance. They said
his blood sugar was causing him weakness. The detectives saw
that he obviously looked sick. Now they have to interview him
again.

Thursday November 2nd 2017,

This %$#@&#! $#!&$. I scream in my head.

HOW AM I SUPPOSED TO HANDLE LIFE RIGHT NOW?
THE EXPLOSIVELY TRAGIC STORY I'M LIVING IS
SICKENING.

Lord help us.

I love the abilities of google. I have someone to ask all of my
crazy questions. Also, note to self: don't google everything.

Saturday November 11th 2017,

Dear, kind, Bryant,

You are no longer mine. That sucks. I'm sad. Thank you for trying for so long. Thank you for generously loving me through the hard time I had while I healed from that car accident in 2015. Thank you for fighting through life with me and for showing me how to chill. Thank you for holding on when I decided after a year and a half of dating you that I wanted to save sex for marriage. Thank you for going to church with me and for truly enjoying it. Thank you for listening to my life-pondering chatter.

It sucks that our relationship evaporated over the phone while I was driving down Highway 212. "I can't do this anymore." You said. And I'm happy you did. I could have selfishly held on to you for forever, even though I've been instructed not to.

"Do not be unequally yoked together with unbelievers." 2 Corinthians 6:14 NKJV

This command is kind. It's stated so that one can be spared of what I did not spare you of, Bryant. When I said yes to dating you, I decided that I'd do what I wanted to do, and that that must be the right thing. I convinced myself that the bible was wrong about who I should be with.

I tried to make up my own rules and fit you into my life, but we kept breaking. I will always hope the best for you. I am amazed that you live looking so brightly at the world as you always have. You are kind, hopeful, you love people who others don't, you laugh like a kid, and I love you.

Sincerely,
Shayla

Sunday November 12th 2017,

6

I am helpless. I can no longer be the one to hold Bryant's hand through earth time. *I pray that one day someone great for him does.*

I am so sad. It's hard to pretend this is all okay. I hate thinking about where on the life-spectrum I am, this might not even be rock bottom. What if this is some middle ground before it gets worse?

Why can't I be happy, contented and THRILLED with the things that I **do** have? What is so terrible about my life anyways? I have a roof over my head and I'm living in a home with some of the most important people in my life (my coworker turned best friend; Benjamin Snow, Helena Giles; Ben's girlfriend [and my close friend], and their beautiful baby Ronin)—they support me, they love me and want the best for me.

Yet here I go again...

My relationship with the most amazing guy just ended. We had three years together, and it doesn't feel wasted. Never have I hoped harder and learned more about life than when I was with Bryant Brown. He made me live for the bigger purpose, even though we didn't live for the same one.

Why must we enter this earth, to live, love, hurt and then die?

It's so confusing down here. You get to choose each of your decisions, and that's annoying. *Since this is all for Your purpose, I would like You to drive all of the time. I'm tired of heartache and sadness and physical pain, AH. I want to live for You. I want to think of myself less, and to serve others effortlessly.*

I would like a husband who's going to come and patch everything up. I would like a husband who will be my glue when I want to scatter my shattered bits all over the place and give up. I want someone to guide me. To undo the patterns that my father created. That I created.

Sad, sad, sad. I'm googling how to fix all of this now.

At Bridgetown church today our pastor John Mark Comer spoke about Jesus and how He really only connected intentionally with twelve people, the rest of His disciples happening along the way. Wow, that's really cool history to remember.

Wednesday November 15th 2017,

Thank-thank-thank the heavenly heavens, I am beginning to see it! I am beginning to see the light at the end of this healing tunnel. God's going to use my pain for others to heal.

Sunday November 19th 2017,

Jami Emerson and I visited First Love Church this evening. Jami is the gift from God who believed me when I told her that I remembered that my dad sexually abused me when I was young. She was the first person I told. I was almost asleep when the memories came back. I was twenty-one. That evening while I walked from my bedroom to the bathroom with a furrowed brow, I realized how afraid I was while I walked around the corners of our home. "I'm twenty-one," I thought. "Why am I so afraid?" I felt the weight of fear on my shoulders, and I wanted it gone. I looked at myself in the mirror and said to God, *"If we have anything else to deal with, I'd like to deal with it. We've already gone through and been fine through the worst of my life."* (I was referencing the physical pain I had endured because of a car accident; that pain was absolutely the worst.) *"I'm ready."* I told Him.

That same evening, right before I fell asleep, a memory flashed behind my eyelids. In it I was tiny. My eyes flew open as I jolted straight up out of my covers. Feelings new to my bones washed over me. In that moment I remembered the bad part of my childhood. And from then on, the holes in the timeline of my life slowly began to fill. I waited a week before I told anyone. I hoped I was crazy for most of that time. I prayed I was. I prayed, *"Lord, even if this did happen, could you make it so that You can erase it?"* I hoped that I had had some sort of mental break, but I couldn't shake the peace that entered my life. Remembering the bad memories made my stomach hurt but after I processed them, I was free. Something left my body every time I delt with a bad memory.

Through prayer and seeking God I knew I had to tell Jami. Her and I have a deep friendship built on the bones of compassion and fire breathing honesty. When we first met, we were both in chronic pain from separate car accidents. She was **literally** my crying buddy. She was the only one who nodded her head and truly knew the pain with me. I was that same consolation for her during that season. She believed me when I told her that I remembered what my dad did to me. She was sad with me. She helped me and encouraged me.

And back to this evening. First Love Church was the most charismatic church experience I have had for sure. The worship there was **free.** Some people were twirling about—some were laughing, and some were enjoying God's presence with their backs on the floor. The speaker, Levi Hug, was visiting from Bethel. His laugh is one of those that makes the joyful burst with laughter—and the angry, angrier. The message he gave about applying the word to our lives was PERFECT.

Then there was what is called a "fire tunnel." The students from Bethel School of Supernatural Ministry lined up and created a tunnel that we walked through while they prayed and laid hands on us.

Uhm.

Yeah.

It was a blur.

A blur of love.

Watching people walk through was beautiful. Some emerged in tears, and some with laughter.

The tunnel seemed to slow the steps of all of its participants.

There is something about encountering the presence of God that slows you down.

I made sure to ask God if it was okay to go through the tunnel (it was something I had never seen or heard of before). I didn't sense a pit-in-my-stomach "no," from the Holy Spirit, so it was a "go" for my tunnel journey.

Uhm.

Yeah.

It was a blur.

A blur of love.

I wrecked by the presence of God in that tunnel. The air was **thick** and almost **hot.** Several of the students (all complete strangers to me) were speaking in tongues (the divine language that God gives His children), and one of them began uttering my name (this did not make me fearful, but rather—it made me conclude that God had to be in control). I couldn't make out what the others were saying, but a woman whose glasses were completely fogged up said to me, "God has given you a vision."

That I'm definitely keeping in my heart pocket.

Only Jami knows that I have received a vision. The details of this picture I have yet to share. I am still wrestling with how to receive all of this...

Monday November 20th 2017,

I spent the day with God speaking and translating tongues. The utterances that came out of my mouth, and the revelations that came up in my heart were beyond me. This was way too cool. There are no words to describe this…

Tuesday November 21st 2017,

Therapy was okay this afternoon. During the session I gave my counselor some vague details of the visions I've been having. I can tell when she thinks I'm coocoo.

Wednesday November 22nd 2017,

I'm jumping to conclusions. The Detective has a family. Is he married? He is just doing his JOB. He has been a light in this situation that I am in with my family, but because of the way he beautifully is I have created a whole future-fantasy-scenario in my head.

Check my heart. Guide me to You, to the path You've laid for me. Pick up my feet from where they need not be. Take the blocks from my peripherals. Let me see more so that I may **know** *more,* **love** *more and* **show up** *more. I give my desires for The Detective to You my King, not because I am hoping for* *him as a reward for giving him up; but because I truly wish to follow Your path.*

Friday November 24th 2017,

I feel depressed today. This might be an attack from the things I have put in my body...

Yesterday
A Poem by Shayla Danielle Laurendeau

I felt more achy than usual

my jaw popped every time I opened it wider than half an inch

so, I took a pain pill.

I was looking for a muscle relaxer, but I guess I'm out.

(It's been over a year and a half since I've needed one.)

Then I wanted to smoke weed, so I did.

Then I ate SO much junk. Not junk **food** but rather, a junk **quantity**. This vicious cycle of overeating to medicate myself binds me.

I feel the slowness of my spirit today.

I need a shift. *God, I'm calling You.*

Tonight, I went to my regular 7PM Sunday attendance at church, and I loved it. The atmosphere at Bridgetown feels like a fresh sunny day in the fall. *God, You were there.* But—this is truly not a season of rejoicing in my spirit, so it's hard to meet new people, especially bright, churchy people. I don't think they've gone through what I'm going through. I'm trying not to compare... I just have **no interest** in attempting to relate to a brother like Cole (whom I met during the four minutes we're punished with to greet the people around us). He chattered on and on about himself. I found myself heavily evaluating him.

Cole, you seem like a nice guy. I'm sorry you have anxiety attacks from the pressure your father puts on your academic success.

He said he had an anxiety attack the other night. Why, in my heartlessness could I not feel empathy for him? I told him to "breathe." That was the best I had. I've had anxiety attacks; I should have been able to relate with him.

It's like I'm mad. It's like I'm mad at my dad that I've had to rewrite my life. He wired my brain with lies. Lies I have to rip up, burn to ashes and let God rewrite.

```
I saw the darkness in him when I was a
little girl. I saw that he was dealing
with painful things that went much, much
deeper than anything I had ever seen.
```

Saturday November 25th 2017,

I'm fatter than I've been in a while. All the excessive food I've been consuming now feels like a self-hate crime.

How I feel from what I nurture my body with is one of the best ways I can love myself. Why would I want to do anything but the **best** for the vessel of my soul? And not to mention—*the temple of Your spirit.*

I want to hear the encouraging words that come from The Detective. I want to call him. It's inspiring to see how he operates, but I confess that my heart is invested. I have no idea what his relationship status is. I need to respect him and have good boundaries.

Sunday November 26th 2017,

Dream

Last night I had a dream that I went to The Detective's office to help him work on something. He was wounded. We were working on some sort of high-priority issue... He had a messed-up jaw, a gash on his head and was limping. Pieces of the ceiling were falling. It looked like an earthquake had happened. I was helping The Detective walk down the hallway. When we passed his boss, he wasn't surprised to see us together. The Detective asked me something about work and I said, "I hadn't really finished it yet." He countered, "The First Lady always finishes her work." And I responded, "I was more so thinking **you** could be the First Lady." Then he grabbed my face and kissed me. "Wow," I said, shocked. "Yeah, it's a little overdue I'd say." He said as he kissed me two more times and explained how we were going to have to be patient for "us."

I just used a bubble-diagram to interpret this dream.

- In the center of the diagram, I wrote who the dream was about (me).
- In sequential order I recorded the big scenes (at the office, walking down the hallway, the dialogue, and the kisses).
- Then I went back through the scenes to note the obvious details.
- Next, I let the Holy Spirit show me God's heart for each scene, recording every detail and symbol that He revealed.
- Then I prayerfully moved through the dream interpreting it's reveals.

The beautiful thing that happened through this interpretation (which I believe God impressed me to do in the first place) was the direction it took me. God revealed to me my earthly, flesh-y desires that I needed to check (the kiss and it being from The Detective). I need to let go of that desire and realize that it's not my time to be with any man. And besides that, The Detective and I have serious work to do, so I hope God can help me wise up with good boundaries quick.

Then something royally rad happened in the middle of the interpretation… I sensed the Holy Spirit say:

What would it look like to create something soon?

And I knew He was talking about the dream I have of building something that repairs the sexually abused. As my heart **swirled,** I realized this business would probably be called, "Diamonds," (a word God has been reminding me of A LOT of lately). Then I got excited, knowing His timing is perfect.

- I **love** the idea of a nonprofit. If the world could run without us having to make money off of each other I would be the most peaceful presence you've ever encountered. But since we are quite far from this happening, I just don't see how I could successfully make a lasting difference creating another nonprofit for the world to donate to.

My mind now wanders to the business model that TOMS uses. They match purchases with great deeds. Whether they donate a pair of shoes or contribute to one of their partnering organizations to end gun violence, restore eyesight or create safe water systems, they have a sustainable way to do a great thing!

But what does my business idea look like? My desire is to enable the abused to find freedom from their abusers…

I'd like to sell one handmade tiara and then crown abuse survivors with a tiara. This is a beautiful idea. And it would be a grand gesture, but is this a lasting crowning? Would that piece of jewelry really be enough for someone to live empowered with the truth of their identity for the rest of their days? (I know this is a big feat I am looking to make, but my audacious visions will not stop.)

I've made jewelry since I was a little girl, the way it looks on me has always helped me feel like the woman I am. I want to give others jewelry so that they can grow into who they were made to be too.

Friday December 1st 2017,

Tonight, I've ended up at Sports on Tap, and this beer concoction I've ordered is the best thing in the world. It's a baked hard apple cider mixed with an Apocalypse IPA. YES.

Friends: I am going to google how to find and make them.

- Get out, do the things you love, and they will come.

The kind waitress here that I know from high school just stopped by and asked me if I was still dating Bryant...

I told her what happened: two different beliefs, coupled up, trying to do life together.

Saturday December 2nd 2017,

To be fearless is to face all of your fears. To face them is to say, "Jesus, I recognize these are not my burdens, show me the truth."

Sunday December 3rd 2017,

Thank You Note to Dad

Thank you,

Dad. for the toxic way you treated me.

Because of your actions I am driven to help stop (and heal) the damage caused by other abusers in this world.

Freedom by truth is coming.

Some of my sad memories remain so unclear.

I'm realizing this might be because I am not meant to remember those moments.

The trust that you made me give you... No wonder I can't trust a human.

Thank you note, over.

```
I have recently been told that parents
rape their children to regain a sense of
power in their life. That makes sense.
That's good to know.

There are too many scars in my body.
```

Monday December 4th 2017,

I thought it was hard listening to God about the stuff He leads us away from... But it is indeed harder trusting Him about the good stuff He calls us to.

I **so badly** want the good stuff. I ask for it, He nudges me there, then suddenly I am fully aware of how undeserving I am.

*I want what You've spoken over me many times in the middle of the night, "Sing," to happen Your way. The right way. I want to surrender **all** even though I want to grab what I want. Show me how to surrender. Show me how to have peace. Show me how to have hope and faith. Show me how to get ready.*

You are getting ready.

Wednesday December 6th 2017,

You would think I'd be lonely, but I'm not. I am happy to continue as is. I am happy to grow more into who I am, who I desire to be and who *You call me to be.*

I am The President of My Life.

Saturday December 9th 2017,

Last night as I was driving home from Jami's I had a pull-over-freak-out meltdown.

God is revealing how hard this season of life will be. It will be a true battle having to stand up to my dad.

The Lord also revealed to me that my deepest feeling right now is fear.

Indeed, but it need not be.

I unblocked my dad's number last night. An impression washed over me to do so, so I did.

Shortly after that I got a text dad sent to Kelsey and I that read, "Girls what can myself and grandma get you for Christmas?"

Deep sigh.

I don't feel like I need to shut you out dad, but I cannot play these mind games. I will not drown **with you** in denial.

I don't want to hold space in my life for these text encounters.

I am speechless.

I am at a loss.

Tuesday December 12th 2017,

Mom, Kelsey and I went out to do festive Christmas activities this evening, and we had a really, really good time. We don't talk about "it." I think we treat dad's actions like diseases that grow if you pay attention to them. We only talk about dad quietly, and no one ever says things perfectly to the others. Kelsey explains that we're in different places, so it's hard to be there for one another. Mom wants to know why, "Why is this happening to us?" And I want to be seen by my family, but also left alone.

Thursday December 14th 2017,

Yesterday I was honest with God about how sad I am. I described to him how distant He's felt lately, and I discovered it's because I let a random article strike fear in me! In the article the writer was explaining the dangers of asking for and then expecting God to give us a "word" or a vision. But after thinking this through I do not think it's a danger! God wants me to ask for and EXPECT His goodness. He never fails. And He loves communication! When I pray, that is time spent with Him while He shapes my heart towards His. And sometimes, when my desires fit into His big plan, my prayers are answered with yeses and moved mountains.

So, about "words" from the Lord…

"So faith comes from hearing, that is, hearing the Good News about Christ." – Romans 10:17 NLT

This verse is talking about hearing the message of Christ as our savior. In its context it seems to be about audibly hearing the good news from another. I've noticed that the Lord spreads the Good News about Christ through others, interferences, words (impressions He puts on your heart) and simply any way He knows we'll listen.

And, about visions...

- I am responsible for testing every word and vision through His word and character.
- I believe He will and does guide me by His spirit.

SO...

After I realized I completely did not agree with the article I read I asked God to show me a vision, or give me a word, if it was His will.

THEN...

Vision

God began to show me a dark underground tunnel. There were three tombstone-like doors… He gave me the impression to "wait." Wait for Him to show me the doors. He said when I am ready they will come, and that there will actually be several doors that I get to choose from. It seemed as though they were all the right choice (and that's just His nature) He often lets us choose. The Detective was standing at my right side. There were many children in the tunnel too. I tried to push The Detective out of the vision (because I thought maybe my heart put him there) but The Detective remained. He stayed after my many requests for the vision to be filled with God's will (not mine). Then I decided: OK, I'll trust this and The Detective's presence being in it.

Then, God asked me to have faith, He said,

Fully leap and wait.

WHAT? He's doing something big.

This Detective thing... *La la la la la.*

Amen to this vision, amen that You speak and hallelujah to Your goodness. God, may You be blessed by those who bless You.

Friday December 15th 2017,

Today I am 12% lonely.

I want more buddies. I want more light. More true friends.

My friendship with my roommate Helena Giles is growing and that's great. I love her. She teaches me often about how to make wise housekeeping and cooking decisions; we've had a lot of laughs about some of the simple things she's taught me. I love her boyfriend and my old boss-turned-best friend Benjamin Snow, and their BEAUTIFUL baby Ronin. Living

21

here with them is great. I love the dogs too, even though they're huge Pitbull's. I'm loved here.

I think that The Detective could be another true friend, but I obviously desire more for that relationship.

I can let go of the desire if I needed to (I sound addicted). What would giving it up look like? *LORD You keep telling me to*

Wait.

You put Your hands on my shoulders and say,

Honey, trust me,

while you let out a knowing, father-laugh like my dad used to do.

It sounds better when You do it.

I miss dad. He wasn't all bad. He was funny and made me feel safe. He was dad-like and fierce when he thought my safety was at stake. Even though he didn't save me from himself.

The other evening Kelsey said, "He's just not who we thought he was." And for me something clicked in that moment. I had been giving my dad two separate beings, the being he was when he was dad, and the being he was when he robbed my innocence.

They are the same human, and as one human, he is broken.

Sunday December 17th 2017,

Dream

Last night I had two dreams, in the first dream I had a realization that The Detective wasn't as cute as I thought, and in the second dream it seemed like I lied to him. We were sitting down, I was describing life to him and he responded with, "Hmm... That's not what you said before."

Interpretation

I believe that the first dream is Jesus demystifying The Detective's attractiveness so that I can get over him. The second dream points out my fear of lying to The Detective about anything that my dad did. The memories from my dad abusing me are a mix of clear, choppy and sick happenings. Happenings so sick that even at my age today I can't see the whole memory for whatever reason God has.

Help me.

Sunday December 24nd 2017,

Dream

Last night I had the season sleeper dream again. It's a dream I get every once in a while, where this crazy-chick sneaks into my old bedroom and sleeps next to me...

Interpretation

There is an extra narrative in my life that needs to go. This woman symbolizes the things that sneak into my intimate spaces. In this dream the woman doesn't bother or frighten me, but she doesn't belong to me. I believe this is a symbol of the narrative of the space-takers in my intimate places.

Is it false wisdom? Since wisdom is portrayed as a woman in the bible, is this woman who sneaks into my bed false wisdom?

Since she's sneaky? Sneaky = not good. Am I inviting false wisdom into my life? Or, is false wisdom going to chronically try to get close to me, like this dream has shown me my whole life? In the end You leave no question unanswered but if for now these are, that's okay.

Lonely, I find myself a little lonely. *I thought we were solving that.* I do wish I had a few more friends to call when funny things happened, or just more people to chat with. I've drawn away from almost everyone who once mattered to me. I either took offence to the way they treated me or found that they were no longer good for my wellbeing. I need to grow in communicating my heart to others… I have found that people sometimes stomp on hearts unknowingly.

I feel like two people. I can wait. I can bravely anticipate the best in any situation. And, I WANT GOOD THINGS NOW. Mmm, I am entitled to different feelings while still being one human.

God, I would like a simpler mindset. You give me exactly what I need. Right now, I need less complexity in my mind. Stress and anxieties love to haunt me. Thank You for the strength You gave me to ask The Detective if he was married. I could have happily continued on, wishing for what was not meant to be, but You enabled me to make the wise move. Amen.

Confessions

I can tell I've been naughty because I need to bullet point my sins.

- *I took my fantasy longings way too far with The Detective. I convinced myself You were guiding me into a relationship with him.*
- *I recently got drunk with my ex-boyfriend, Damian, and almost had sex with him. There is no wise reason*

24

for me to keep him in my life. Most of what he symbolizes to me is a confused adolescence.

- *God, I sexualize a lot of my male connections, always assuming the hottest fire of romantic relations.*

Today's feeling of lack of oxygen in my body reminds me of moments with my father. Trying to find breath, trying to steady breath, trying to understand why it was hard to breathe.

Monday December 24rd 2017,

Dream

I had a dream last night that the devil was trying to catch me doing wrong, but I was walking fully in the light.

He sought unsuccessfully.

Interpretation

Amen. That's the goal.

Tuesday December 25th 2017,

Last Night I was in my feelings and my pain, so I skipped a Christmas Eve party to smoke weed by myself. Then the night got worse.

All night I fought fear.

I had a dream I was being raped all night. I kept waking up from it.

It was as if evil spirits were trying to rob my sanity.

Merry Christmas.

Did I do this to myself? Was my solo sad party an open invitation for demons?

Wednesday December 26th 2017,

I have been stalling writing a **real** journal entry because I dread facing the shame that's attached to my present struggles…

I have been **daily** recalling how much of my body I have abused willingly with boyfriends, parties, and clothing attire.

I was so naive.

There were times I was intoxicated enough to convince my morals they were fine to die so I could guiltlessly continue on. *I repent of these times, Father. Set me free.*

Paranoia likes to sit in, attacking me. She drives fake fears to outrageous extents… She's annoying.

I have to cry out.

I pray for guidance. For truth. Some paranoia shifts to intuition as truth is revealed. Some paranoia burns in holy fire to be gone **forever,** proved to be lies that were created to deter me.

On Christmas Eve I ditched mom and Kelsey. This time of year gets to me.

I am weighed by the heavy pressure of the holidays. How am I supposed to celebrate right now?

I chose not to be with even one person.

God, I am just a little human! Why does so much happen in my life?!

In one moment, I had myself believing I was destined to be with The Detective. I was swimming in daydreams of a future with him. And, in the very next moment I got myself wrapped into a situation with Damian (that I disobediently walked into) even AFTER God whispered,

We're not going there.

Since God knew I **would not listen** to His gentle pressing, He probably permitted the enemy's will to happen to my jaw. Here's how it went down: I was at a creative's meet-up with my beautiful friend Rosa Reyna, and my jaw was **really** hurting. I ended up leaving because I could hardly engage in conversation. I sat in my car for a while massaging my face and texting an old friend, my ex-boyfriend, Damian.

Not safe.

You began to whisper.

We were messaging about our plans later. I told him my jaw was out of its socket and that I wasn't sure I'd be up for catching up. Then the Holy Spirit spoke,

We're not going there.

But I continued on with my plan making.

Damian's reply was a red-flag innuendo that drew me back. That wasn't the Damian I knew.

Maybe my jaw slid out of socket so I'd take the extra hint and skip meeting him.

Nonetheless, in defiance I decided to start drinking to see if it'd feel better, because why would God ever want to guard me from an old boyfriend?

God... Allow me to hold Your whispers tighter. Wholly, never with a grain of salt. I ask that I take the whole rock of salt that is your command and swallow it happily, with minimal heartburn afterwards.

I heard You say "No," not to hang out with him. And I felt my jaw as it caused me more and more pain in the hours before seeing him.

I'm sorry. Please forgive me.

Friday December 29th 2017,

I just had a vision of Damian and I surrendering our lives to Your purpose. Is this true? God is this You? Would You reveal it to me if so? Guide more than my heart this time. Guide my reasoning. Guide me to You. Bring needed growth areas to the forefront of my mind. Why must You make me surrender so deeply? I have already said I give it all to You.

Sad Poem
By Shayla Laurendeau

Maybe this picture is You showing me
That we surrender our lives to You

Separately.

Sunday December 31st 2017,

Am I crazy for wanting to go to The Detective, to tell him that I doubt myself and that I'm not sure if my memories about dad are real?

They don't feel real.

Why are we here?

Why are we at this point in healing?

Wasn't doubt supposed to be a thing of the past, something to hilariously laugh at now? I know, remember and feel what happened to me, but my dad says differently. He says, "This didn't happen." And it eats me.

I am lonely. Very lonely.

It was hard telling Jami my life's dream yesterday. That look on her face. I think I saw every emotion. Shock; disbelief, belief, excitement, growth, and her maturity. All in one moment.

Stop acting with each other.

I surrender. This is me, not conceptualizing who I need to be.

I would eat **so** much as a child. Shortly after my dad left my body alone, I found time to feel the pain. At nine years old I had myself eating and eating and eating.

Are you willing to bet on "it" working? Are you willing to bet on me working? Will you make room for the space I want to make for you?

The gift You're bringing me is bigger than a lot. God, You're saying,

It's bigger. It's larger. It's grander, there's more. There's more to be expected. More to be desired.

The guy I am waiting for... His existence is becoming less and less a stress to wait for and more and more a blessing I am going to receive **well,** *THANK YOU GOD.*

My guy will be a conqueror of this time. That's for sure.

Looking back now I wonder if some part of me was really caring about Damian all these years…

Well, of course I was. A boyfriend is a boyfriend is a boyfriend, right?

Quiet Time
A Short Story by Shayla Laurendeau

God,

     Life is sweeter when I give everything to You. I used to give You little. I ran from the hurt and wouldn't let You come and fill me like You promise to.

I was weak. All my mind could feel was the weight of what I let no one else carry with me.

I used to feel unworthy in my church-life.

I felt less-than-glorious as a child of God.

"They don't get **it**." I would think to myself. "The Church people around me don't know how viciously my insides eat me."

I felt too prideful in my outside-of-church-life.

"They don't get **it**." I thought. "The non-believing humans think they're living for only earth time. That's preposterous."

And where did this young, tortured believer go?

Running. I stopped trying to think through my decisions. I didn't know how to live in the space between believing in God and psychologically unable to grasp how to live the right life for Him when I was angry about the demons who worked so hard at pressing me down.

Years rolled by and so did sins, "Please forgive me's" and wild times.

Then a car accident in 2015 broke me (like the way you tame a horse).

The pain I was in made me so miserable that I was willing to finally let go. I thought, "If the way my life has been going has anything to do with me not doing the few things I know I need to do in order to follow God fully, then I'm all in." I decided: no more premarital sex, no more party drugs. And as I resisted the devil he began to flee from my life. His exit was a slow departure, that's for sure. He wouldn't get the hint, so I packed his things for him.

LORD, I'm listening. And if I'm not, quiet my heart, my mind and my mouth.

```
I've been ignoring my dad's texts... What
else am I supposed to do?
```

Monday January 1st 2018,

I don't know who came up with the stages of grief, but they got it all wrong... I've circled back to denial more than once.

Dream

Last night I had a dream a female friend and I had sex...

Interpretation

Lord, I receive this as a warning to stop perverting myself with this person. This friendship is the **last thing** from sexual. Especially because it's a woman in my life. *But if the way I engage in this relationship is fading my purity, show me the right way to engage in it.*

Happy New Year.

Tuesday January 2nd 2018,

Dream

Last night I dreamt about Austin, a kid I went to elementary school with. Then the dream shifted subjects to a man who took me on a long date and then tried to have sex with me. He gawked when I didn't.

*Father, rise up a generation of stoked abstinence-practicing creations. Let us enjoy the abundant fruitfulness of sex **within marriage.***

To be a million percent honest I occasionally smoke weed to release my anxieties. I secretly hate this place (earth).

My body is suffering because of the car accidents and abuse I've suffered… It's a bummer here.

God You make me dig to the root so You can completely pluck out every deep pain.

```
It's    sad    that    men    and    women    doing
pedophiliac acts hide in the church (or
anywhere).
```

```
What happens when you give-give-give to
the devil?
```

```
When does he own you?
```

```
At times as a little human I was wound
into a state of psychosis hypnosis… Dad
repeated things over and over and over
until I didn't believe otherwise.
```

Thursday January 4th 2018,

It's 6:53AM and I have a cold so I should be in bed but I'm sitting at Starbucks because I woke from a nightmare.

Well, it wasn't as much of a nightmare as it was a dream of a party. It was for my birthday (or a celebration of something I did).

Dream

Dad was gone this time. It was only mom parenting us. Kelsey wasn't there. I threw a party with Ben, Helena and lots of my friends (a lot of them were actually Ben and Helena's friends). Then people from high school started to show up, and the house got bigger. I felt bad for mom because all of my friends were keeping her up. Most people's dogs came with them too.

I was lying in my old bed, paralyzed, so tired. A few people kept coming in and out of my room. I suddenly felt someone lying next to me, and immediately I said, "WHO IS THAT?" It was some random chick, saying she had a blood-sugar thing going on, so she needed to lie down. I calmed down then I got up out of bed (not looking so hot).

I started to wander around, trying to figure out how to calm the commotion down. I told my mom I was handling it, but I wasn't actually telling anyone to quiet down. I was observing. I felt like I wanted to be helpless, I didn't desire to be the authoritative figure that needed to tell people to leave.

As I moved through the house it turned into a gymnasium and more and more people from high school showed up. I saw Bryant and his friends gathered around couches on what looked like a TV set. I felt like avoiding him and I did, which was weird.

As I continued to walk, I saw Tim Davis, our family's pastor, chatting with some people. I was pulled away from him by someone, so I continued to walk.

The chaos started to calm down… And then I saw Michael, a man from grade school, and he was a reprieve for me. I dove into his arms for an embrace, it felt good—but not right. He started to pull away from me, but I kept holding him. He continued to hug me but then started to kiss my neck. I pulled back once I realized what was happening and slapped him. Then I flipped him off (and felt bad doing it). I could have willed not to do it, but I didn't.

When I pulled away from Michael his face was different than when I walked up to him. He now had all devilish details. Glossy red eyes glowed through his stretched facial features. He shrugged his shoulders, mumbling something along the lines of, "It's my will…"

Then I whipped my head and body **180° away** from him, and as I did, I was embodied with a **weightless strut.** Then there was no one else as I walked on, I was at the end of the **gymnasium.**

Suddenly I was pulled into what felt like a more conscious, darker place of dreaming. Everything lost color. I was lying with my back on my childhood bed and someone was dragging back the corners of my mouth while robbing the breath from my lungs through the back of my body.

I thought, "satan himself," and knew I couldn't fight this on my own. I rasped "God save me! Jesus! Help Me! Jesus, by your pow…"

Then I was woken by the sound of one of my roommates getting ready for work this morning, I was thankful for the commotion.

God I am going to ask You to interpret this dream if You'd like to.

Interpretation

I have bolded ideas that feel significant to me in order to interpret this dream well. And I had the idea to interpret it by breaking it up piece by piece, using personal commentary and Holy Spirit-led reveals.

*Spirit of God, take over my mind and my heart's intentions right now. Show me how to hear You through **every bit** of this* *dream. Lord, reveal Your intentions to me. Jesus, protect me, heal my heart. I leave all of my predispositions at Your feet. Amen.*

Dad was gone this time. It was only mom parenting us. **Kelsey wasn't there.**

- *I believe this is You touching on... The future or present tense of my family.*
- Kelsey not being there references her not being involved in this particular situation.

I threw a party with Ben, Helena and lots of my friends (a lot of them were actually Ben and Helena's friends). Then people from high school started to show up, and the house got bigger. I felt bad for mom because all of my friends were keeping her up. **Most people's dogs came with them too.**

- Utter chaos... Any place where dogs are there too is chaos.

I was lying in my teenage bed, **paralyzed,** so tired.

- This **paralyzed** feeling makes me draw a connection to the one time on this bed when my dad assaulted me, paralyzing my body and my rationality.

A few people kept coming in and out of my room. I suddenly felt someone lying next to me, and immediately I said, "WHO IS THAT?" It was some random chick, saying she had a **blood-sugar thing** going on, so she needed to lie down. I calmed down then I got up out of bed **(not looking so hot).**

-   The fact that this woman had a **blood-sugar thing** going on reiterates the connection of this woman symbolizing my type 1 diabetic father.

- Me **not looking so hot** makes me remember that sad moment in that same room with the same pink stripe paint in the dream as the last time my dad sexually abused me when I was 15. I was drugged up after I had my wisdom teeth out. Clearly portraying a disheveled appearance.

I started to wander around, trying to figure out how to calm the commotion down. **I told my mom I was handling it,** but **I wasn't actually telling anyone to quiet down.**

-   I did not tell **anyone to quiet down** at this age, not my friends, not my party buddies, nor my abusive father.
-   I also kept my mom out of the loop about the abuse I suffered because I thought I should handle the darkness without her. That lie (that I should handle it without my mother) is reiterated here when **I told my mom I was handling it,** when really, I wasn't.

I was observing. I felt like **I wanted to be helpless**, I didn't desire to be the authoritative figure that would tell people to leave.

-   **I wanted to be helpless,** I didn't want to be the hero for myself. Maybe for some reason it wasn't yet time to conquer fearlessness at that time. Now, I cannot deny the authority I have over my life.

As I moved through the house it turned into a gymnasium and more and more people from high school showed up. I saw **Bryant** and his friends gathered around couches on what looked like a TV set. I felt like avoiding him and I did, which was weird.

- This touches on me having boundaries that are healthy for my healing process right now, amen.

As I continued to walk, I saw **Tim Davis** chatting with some people. I was **pulled away** from him by someone, so I continued to walk.

- **Tim Davis,** pastor and friend, makes me think of wholeness, a heart seeking Yours.
- The motion of me being **pulled away** from wholeness highlights spiritual warfare. Only the enemy would want me in a place away from wholeness.

The chaos started to calm down… And then I saw **Michael** and he was a reprieve for me. I dove into his arms for an embrace, it felt good—but not right. He started to pull away from me, but I kept holding him. He continued to hug me but then started to kiss my neck. I pulled back once I realized what was happening and slapped him. **Then I flipped him off** (and felt bad doing it). **I could have willed not to do it, but I didn't.**

- The name Michael means "who is like God?"
- This makes me think that I treat people like they're God when I never should. I think that point is driven home because of the specific relationship I have with **Michael.** He's a kind man I went to school with, elementary through high school. He was always kind to me, and always safe. If I saw him today, I'd go in for a hug like I did in my dream.
- I treat people like they can be my haven or my safety.
- Only God should be my safety, people are mine only to love. People can't part the waters for me when I'm running from my enemies. People can't make the rain fall when I want to feel the comfort of an Oregon rainy day. Humans are wonderfully loving and purposed, but not one of them will be my safe haven.

- **Then I flipped him off** makes me think of the fierceness I feel when something is not right. Flipping someone off is not a natural reaction for me, it's not even in my demeanor vocabulary. It makes me think of being at a total loss. If I were ever to be (I won't be) caught flipping someone off, it'd be because they did something demonically awful.
- **I could have willed to do it, but I didn't.** This makes me think of not having self-control, even when being wronged. *Oh Lord, train me.*

When I pulled away from Michael his face was different than when I walked up to him. He now had all **devilish details.** Glossy red eyes glowed through his stretched facial features. He shrugged his shoulders, mumbling something along the lines of, "It's my will…"

- These **devilish details** are a reminder that the allure of safety here on earth is just that, an allure. The safety that we soothe ourselves with can switch into a hell.

Then I whipped my head and body **180° away** from him, and as I did, I was embodied with a **weightless strut.** Then there was no one else as I walked on, I was at the end of the **gymnasium.**

- Because I turned away from this devil-like figure and became weightless (like you are when demons leave your life) I think of: "Resist the devil and he will flee from you." James 4:7. AMEN.
- The **gymnasium** symbolizes the range of strength I need to exercise; telling people what Jesus would, resisting hanging with ex boyfriends, not treating people like God, and standing firm when entities try to pull me away from God.

Suddenly I was pulled into what felt like a more conscious, **darker place** of dreaming.

- Only because God knew I could handle it.
- "I have told you these things, so that in me you may have peace. In this world you will have trouble. But take heart! I have overcome the world." John 16:33 NIV

Everything lost color. I was lying with my back on my childhood bed and someone was **dragging back the corners of my mouth** while **robbing my breath** from the back of my body.

I thought, **"satan himself,"** and knew I couldn't fight this on my own. I rasped **"God save me! Jesus! Help Me! Jesus, by your pow…"**

- When someone is **dragging back the corners of** your mouth, you're in pain and it's manipulatively demonic.
- My breath has been robbed. I still have trouble breathing. *Jesus help me.*
- My breath often left me while I laid on this bed as a little girl. This was a side effect of dissociating while my dad was messing with me.
- **"satan himself,"** is a picture of exactly whose plans these were. satan comes to steal, kill and destroy.

"The thief comes only to steal and kill and destroy; I have come that they may have life, and have it to the full." – John 10:10 NIV

One might ask, if Jesus comes to give us life, and to have it to the full, why would He let satan have his way, and allow a little girl to be raped? You'll see. Just like I'll see. God has a plan past what we're doing now. If I suffered here so that my eternity rocks, then amen. If I suffered here so that I could learn first-hand

40

compassion, then amen. If I suffered here so I could understand as much of God as I was intimately designed to, then halleluiah. I count it all as gain.

"God save me! Jesus! Help Me! Jesus, by your pow…"

- This was the cry in my spirit as a young girl. I never formed those words, but I felt them.
- I remember one particular night when I was eight or nine, things started to click, and I felt like the relationship my dad and I had was wrong. My heart was pounding in my stomach as I thought about asking him if we could stop. I didn't know what to say or how to, or if I could. I didn't have time to breathe. I was scared of disappointing my dad, so I never spoke up. My voice was suffocated. But shortly after this, the Lord moved. My dad came into my bedroom one night when I was nine years old. He sat on my bed and told me we couldn't do what we've been doing anymore.

Friday January 5th 2018,

Everything that happens around us is a glowing invitation to grow for something greater than us.

Dream

There was some sort of demonic ritual happening, I wasn't involved in it, but I was near it. I lived in a grander house. In my dream I took in the surroundings of my room then went to sleep. I "woke up" to a faint hissing sound and looked at the stove top that was in my room. All of the burners were on and the plastic decor hanging on the wall was melting. I tried to turn the stove's knobs off but all they did was turn and turn. The whole unit seemed like it was about to blow. I knew evil spirits were messing with me. I tried to figure out

41

what else I could do but I was helpless. The dream was like a game show. As I tried to leave the room I rasped to Helena for help (I knew I wasn't going to be able to get out of the room by myself).

There was no door handle, so she put her baby Ronin down then busted the door in. We then ran around the house for the rest of the dream. I explained to her what happened, and she reacted with an, "Ahh." I replied, "No, I know no one would've broken in, I would've woken up, right? This was satan himse…" Then I cut my sentence short because it truly felt like the wrong thing to say, like it wasn't the truth.

LORD. I type and my heart asks, are these dreams revealing something to me? Are You saying something here? I am not afraid in them, there is no need to be. So, what are we doing here?

I have the impression to speak tongues and then translate it right now…

Faith will get you further than you dream. Have hope in me.

I wonder what would happen if you surrendered it all.

If flowers would bloom to their full capacity; there would be no wait.

Why wait for the full capacity, the full allowance? Travel now. Serve now. Wait now.

Why did what You brought to me through the translation of tongues have little to do with my dream?

Saturday January 6th 2018,

Dream

Last night I had a nightmare of a huge cabin I had all to myself. There was someone else there, but I never saw them. Drawers were being opened and then shut and then opened. I ran around the kitchen corner to find the presence, but I never saw them.

I pray against the enemy distracting me with his drawer opening and shutting. Lord, I wait patiently for You to open the door. I don't need drawers to store my belongings, I need You, the doorkeeper.

Sunday January 7th 2018,

I remember a nice night when Kelsey and I were younger, and we stayed the night with Elizabeth. I remember feeling an overwhelming sense of safety in her and her family's home.

My young mind tried to conceptualize how to tell Elizabeth's dad about dad. I wondered if I could tell him, or if I could tell Elizabeth's mom, and what I would say…

That evening I stayed silent, and while Kelsey and Elizabeth were asleep, I sat at the top of the staircase thinking, thinking, thinking. My young eyes peered through the dark at all the different pictures of Elizabeth that hung on the walls.

Friday January 12th 2018,

Dad,

You intentionally robbed me of my innocence, therefore you willingly stripped yourself of yours. Last night I **mourned** for you. You must feel heavily burdened, as do I. An unbearable darkness sits on your lap and it's nothing that can evaporate.

I mourn for you.

Every soul in human existence grows up with a broken will. Regardless, we **must** train it. That's what makes the justice-lovers so bold, we FIGHT.

It's flooring, the man who guided the foundation of my spiritual journey was and is leading a life exactly opposite of what he verbally taught me to do. But I am **done** trying to wrap my mind around that—I will be wiser now.

I watched you… All those years. I saw the sneakiness and the red flags. I saw lies in your eyes.

To them I pay no longer mind.

Sow for Your Creator
A Devotional by Shayla Laurendeau

In my studies in James today it reads, **"Now listen, you who say, 'Today or tomorrow we will go to this or that city, spend a year there, carry on business and make money.' Why, you do not even know what will happen tomorrow. What is your life? You are a mist that appears for a little while and then vanishes. Instead, you ought to say, 'If it is the LORD's will, we will live and do this or that. As it is, you boast in your arrogant schemes. All such boasting is**

44

evil. If anyone, then, knows the good they ought to do and doesn't do it, it is a sin for them." James 4:13-16 NIV

My thoughts are peaceful about this passage. I sow into today for the hope of harvest tomorrow. I feel challenged to write a devotional that has my interpretations shorter than each passage of the word. Here I go:

"Now listen, you who say, 'today or tomorrow we will go to this or that city, spend a year there, carry on business and make money.' 14 Why, you do not even know what will happen tomorrow."

Hope for things with the Lord. Go for things with the Lord. Keep your heart open as you work on the good things He's put in front of you. But stay tuned, He might derail you for His better plan.

"What is your life? You are a mist that appears for a little while and then vanishes."

Each of us was important enough for God to create, but we are vapor without Him.

"Instead, you ought to say, 'If it is the LORD's will, we will live and do this or that."

To be set on our uncertain plans is to deny the peace of His perfect direction.

"As it is, you boast in your arrogant schemes. All such boasting is evil. If anyone, then, knows the good they ought to do and doesn't do it, it is a sin for them."

Lord, let us stay humble to follow Your plans. Let us stay humble to be obedient to follow Your plans.

Saturday January 13th 2018,

God, heal my father… He needs to journey out of the nasty that he's lived in.

*Cement in me THE TRUTH. If I am dragging around anything that is displeasing to You, bring it to the center of my mind so we can **deal with it.***

Right now, I have an acronym for working through the repressed memories that came back:

T... Talk it out
W... Write it out
A... Allow the memory to pass through my body
P... Pray away the lies, and for restoration
D... Do an intentional prayer for healing or some listening yoga (listening to God's prompts for the movements)

TWAPD, because I feel trapped, until we go through this acronym.

*Lord, I come to you in humility… I am really **not** sure how to accept the worthiness you say I have. I can't help but remember the things I've done that make me feel less than worthy of a good life… I ask, and BEG for freedom from this. I don't want this to be my forever. Do I have to travel through every unknown to feel and see the truth? I need to have peace in the undiscovered, always knowing **You** are the truth. My answer, **all** truth. I love You. Free me. Please.*

Tuesday January 16th 2018,

Jami is on her way to a vacation in Hawaii right now. Then to Australia, indefinitely. Yesterday was difficult, saying goodbye. On my drive home I pulled over and sobbed for a while and made a wildly emotional recording on my phone.

The divine timing of my friendship with Jami will always be remembered as irreplaceable. She believes in me.

Friday January 26th 2018,

I have an abundance of love right now. I am filled with gratitude. The Lord has been so faithful to me as we journey closely. He is blessing every direction I seek Him in. Everything I ask for, He's granting.

I am assuming this is true when it aligns with His will.

LORD, **let me see Your will** *so I can ask for what should be for me and for others. I seek clarity, clarity, clarity for the path I go. Thank You for the desire of faithfulness to You that You have planted in me.*

Saturday January 27th 2018,

The Detective says that he believes that God helps children by sometimes causing them not to be able to remember abuse they suffered.

LORD, I pray that I live my life with eyes locked on You.

Thursday February 1st 2018,

Note to self: don't make your to-do's a greater priority than your neighbors.

The tendons on the back of my neck have finally healed. My head now feels rightly attached to my body. AMEN. I needed this today. The lack of healthy body mass I've had since that car accident has been more than enough to make me feel sorry for myself. But today, I'm shedding some of that damage.

In my closeness with God, I live so far away from the worries of this world.

Wednesday February 15th 2018,

"Defend your light with your life." - Will Smith

Saturday February 17th 2018,

1 Corinthians 13:1, "If I speak in the tongues of men or of angels, but do not have love, I am only a resounding gong or a clanging cymbal."

Friday February 23rd 2018,

Dream

I had a nightmare last night that a friend of mine was lying on me, raping me. I was trying to push him off of me, but I had no strength, nor could I speak. My mouth felt like chalk. My left ankle was pinned under his heavy leg. He was physically heavier than he is in real life. It was torture. I hated the look on his face. I hated that he wasn't hearing me. My left ankle needed to be free, so I squirmed and squirmed and squirmed, but then I felt him get heavier.

I felt God say to my heart, "It's me…" And then my foot got free right before I was about to pass out. I grabbed a pot and whacked my friend repeatedly, but had zero strength. I don't think I made a solid hit. Then I picked up a phone and dialed 911. While it rang, I thought about my friend getting in trouble, and then I cancelled the call.

Then I woke up.

Interpretation

I cancelled the call in my dream just like I cancelled speaking up when I was little. I didn't tell my mom about my dad abusing me until last year, because my dad explained to me when I was young that he'd get in trouble. He even had a lady cop come to the house and talk to me, explaining the trouble he could get in. It probably wasn't a real cop. We were in my parent's bedroom. The cop and my dad were sitting on the bed. I was sitting on the hope chest at the foot of the bed. It was a short conversation. One that felt was wrong. But as a child, I was being told that I had to protect my dad for what he'd done to me. The reasoning didn't click, but I obeyed.

Wednesday March 7th 2018,

God is refining me to be a Christ-like individual.

I am growing to **thrive** in the midst of tough situations, and to tolerate (and love) less-than-tolerable things.

RELEASE the crazy. Release the me that says things that are ***out-there.*** *Release the statements I say that are* ***wildly*** *true because* ***You are*** *capable. Free me.*

The pain in my body is not mine to hold for any reason other than to glorify You.

I am RICH, CONTENTED and HAPPY with what I have.

The incontinence... I was **lucky** if I didn't pee myself in elementary school or at play dates. I wet my pants through the third grade. I always wet myself then had to hide it... I'd wrap sweatshirts around myself, etc. It's no coincidence that the incontinence stopped when the abuse stopped.

49

Tuesday March 13th 2018,

Talk
Write
Allow
Pray
Do

He would shove it all the way down my throat.

He suffocated me.

Another time my pubic bone was so injured that I had to go to the doctor.

As a little girl I told our family physician: "The pain is right here," pointing to my inner left thigh, too embarrassed to have him check out the real source of my pain: the special place on my pubic bone, feeling shattered and on fire.

How was I supposed to explain to him where the injuries came from?

Father I hear You now as You whisper, *Follow me to Mexico.*

I wonder what that means. Should I move out? Ah. Ah.

Yes; because child... You'll progress at such an invaluable rate, you'll love yourself in me.

I need scripture.

50

"Because of that experience, we have even greater confidence in the message proclaimed by the prophets. You must pay close attention to what they wrote, for their words are like a lamp shining in a dark place—until the Day dawns, and Christ the Morning Star shines in your hearts." 2 Peter 1:19 NLT

"Have I not commanded you? Be strong and courageous. Do not be terrified, do not be discouraged, for the Lord your God will be with you wherever you go." Joshua 1:9 NIV

Am I going to Mexico?

Friday March 16th 2018,

What if I bought a whole apartment building and hired people to hold healing sessions in each space?

YAY.

Saturday March 17th 2018,

My eyes are green. No pinching me please. Happy Saint Patrick's Day.

I checked out the one bedroom that my coworker Jen Coffman is moving out of. I would LOVE to live there. She has the **set up.**

I would get to park right outside of the home's entrance **and** rent is cheaper than anywhere else around here. Plus, it's a month-to-month lease! So, I've cancelled my move-in plans at Brooklyn Yard.

Brooklyn Yard is a beautiful apartment building with industrial looking details and clean and open apartments, but I was too anxious in my daydreams about living there. Rent was going to be $1350 a month, and all I could envision was me **hustling** to make it work. I have enough money from the insurance settlement from the car accident to make it work for a while—but then what?

It was going to be a life of trying-trying-trying to get money made.

*I know though, that I **heard** Your voice when I pulled up to Brooklyn Yard the first time. I heard You say,*

This is home.

But it's so expensive...

Sunday March 18th 2018,

I'm feeling awful, I think it's about my move. Something is off about it. God's whispering,

Don't you think I can do better? What do you want?

I want sleep.
I want rest.
I want peace.
I want to dive into health coaching.
I want to follow God's guidance.
I want physical health.
I want to stop being so irritated by certain humans…

So, what makes most sense is to move into Jen's perfect place where I can nest up for however long I need.

Sell all your things. We're going to Mexico.

I hear You, and I write it down… I have to keep going. I can do this while I'm at Jen's. Dwindle my belongings down and take time to be Shayla.

Maybe You want me to hear about Your plans to take me to Mexico so that I am free to go there when it's time. Maybe You're telling me to sell all of my things so that I can be ready to leave when it's time.

God in writing and in my heart, I ask that You put a heavy blanket over me and everything around me. I'm cold. Though, I'm not breaking. Let me be stronger, even more courageous, and diligent. You've lit my passion for You—please don't let me let anything rain on it. Thank You. For all of it.

I feel awful because my dad's in the hospital because of sickness. Oh, diabetes. They say something is wrong with his gallbladder? Yeah, right. Something is wrong with his soul.

Tuesday March 27th 2018,

I had a terrible dream last night. It didn't scare me but [bleh] it gave me an icky feeling. The scene was similar to that of the one in the movie "Holes." In it I was trying-trying-trying to solve things, and I felt like I was "on-the-go."

Dream

I was sitting in the bottom of a dry moat that wrapped around a big piece of land. I was topless, in leggings. An older man walking with a cane approached me. He was above me on the ground level. I was thinking: "No, no, no" (while I recognized that I was topless). He looked at all my strewn about stuff (cash, clothes, and trinkets) and jokingly said, "Oooh, I'd like one of those hundred-dollar bills."

I thought he was kidding but possessiveness radiated out of me as I angrily replied, "No."

He looked at me then I kind of tripped and he greedily hissed, "Oh, I didn't notice you were topless."

"No!" I screamed. He started to crawl into the moat as I desperately attempted my escape... I moved so quickly that I beat him out before he climbed in. He lunged towards my chest with his mouth open and I took the blanket (that I randomly had) and tossed it over his head, kicking him into the moat.

His neck cracked and he died.

The dream shifted and I told mom and Kelsey, "The worst thing that has ever happened to me happened." They were scared when I told them, but so proud that I kept myself safe. They weren't even mad about me randomly being topless, which was nice.

Oh, the colors of night's thoughts.

Tears stream down my face as I realize this dream's meanings. God's asking me to write the interpretation down on paper. Some things aren't for everyone to see. I'll be back soon.

I don't know if anyone notices how strange some of my mannerisms are.

I hold my face back from expressing full emotions because of the pain... I don't want to have pain at the end of the day from overexerted facial use...

I have so much anger inside of me from my history of unwanted touches... It is most obvious to me while Scout and Alice (Ben and Helena's dogs) try to jump on me... I'm not a fan of people or dogs being all up in my space when I don't want it.

Thursday March 29th 2018,

Dream

Last night I had a dream that I bought a house, and Kelsey and our deceased family dog, Pepsi were there. Pepsi was fat and walking around. Our neighbors (there were lots of them who lived in one house) persistently invited us over to their place.

All the neighbors had symbolic bracelets on.

Both houses were large, ours had only framework and flooring while our neighbors had a few more finished details. We were all hanging out on the higher floors, able to see into the unfinished houses.

I had Kelsey wait for me to swing over first. I strapped myself to a bungee cord with which I impressively did a backflip into their house with.

The feeling was that we were in a bad circumstance, but doing the leap was inevitable. So, I went first then tossed her the rope, cheering her on.

Saturday March 31st 2018,

I'm beginning to use my Holistic Health Coach training from Institute of Integrative Nutrition to build clientele! Today I had my first Health History Consultation with a yoga student of mine, Amanda. It went really well! The meeting flowed with ease—until I was choppy, and my confidence evaporated while I listed my prices at the end.

My lack of confidence stems from:
- Assuming people can't afford the personally tailored health services I offer.
- Me not realizing the value I can add to the client...
- Feeling the desperate draw to accumulate money, which is a LIE. I don't need to store up large sums of money. I trust that I'll be taken care of. I always am.

What I **can** have full confidence in is:
- The value I add to my client's wellbeing.
- My desire to help heal people from the inside out.
- That I will consistently give this and ALL of my work 100% effort.

Sunday April 2nd 2018,

I taught yoga (my day job) hungover this morning from the nearly two-box cookie freak-out I had last night...

Church was great last night. *I felt ready to say "Yes, yes, yes," to whatever You wanted to send my way. I asked You to speak to me about whatever You wanted me to work towards. Whatever You wanted to communicate; I was all ears.*

Will you believe me?

You prompted.

YES. I spoke.

Right then, we drove past the Brooklyn Yard apartments, and I sensed You say,

I wanted you there.

And I had a vulnerable Lala freak-out to Your response.

Indeed, I believed You.

*And it was **too much** for me, so I got sugar to get the only legal Christian high.*

I spent the whole box and three quarters of another looking at the cheapest apartments in Portland that I could find (that were cute, with parking, community patios and individual balconies).

"Because if God wants me downtown," my insides said, "okay great fine, but I want the amenities that bring me peace in all that populated cluster-mania."

I will trust You and step out as I experiment with finding higher-paying health coaching clients downtown. Lead me to see the vision through. I LOVE YOU. I want to live a life of stepping out. Of GOING.

Thank You for technology so that I can write in The Healing Diary while I wait for my pelvic ultrasound appointment.

God, I pray for Your will to be done—and for this appointment to bring peace, guidance, and answers… I'm worried about the damage that has been done to me.

Monday April 3rd 2018,

I am beyond tired. I'm thankful that today is my day off. It saddens me that this exhaustion is normal.

Before dreams last night, I gave my intentions to God, saying, *"Okay, I'm here, I'm awake, let's keep doing this, let's dive in and get all of the memories from the abuse out..."* And I kept getting to the tip of a memory but then my body drifted to sleep...

Because of all of the things that have been done to my body I've been wanting to get checked to make sure my reproductive organs are okay. During my ultrasound yesterday, the nurse found no alarming masses (AMEN). She only found a single two-and-a-half-centimeter cyst on my right ovary. She said those can sometimes come and go with your menstrual cycle. Well, that one's going to hang out for a while because I haven't had my period in four months. I think it's because of stress. Helena wisely explained to me, "Your body will assess what's going on and shut down your baby-making abilities because it'll just know you cannot have a baby right now."

That's cool. Good.

Sex is how you make a baby also, body, so—I wasn't going to do that.

Regardless, thank you: body, for adjusting to circumstances.

AND I didn't google anything about cysts on ovaries, so ten peace points for me.

Thursday April 6th 2018,

I am thankful for my health. I am thankful that for my field of work I work out and teach others how to do so as well. Teaching yoga is fun. Each class invites me into serenity's embrace. Growing your body through a physical diligence can cause you to surpass self-set and external-set limits.

*Thank you, Jesus, for the help You gave today so I could wake up refreshed **regardless** of the fact that sleeping was not much of a thing last night. I acknowledge that I drank caffeinated kombucha in the afternoon, so I am sure that had something to do with it...*

Yesterday's supine matsyasana and baddha konasana were **crazy**. I was lying back with a pillow under my upper spine, knees bent, legs opened, feet pressing together and soft blocks under each knee... And God met me.

I tried to let my body relax as best as I could then He whispered,

Are you going to trust what's about to happen?

I said "*Yes...*" and seconds later it felt like my left leg was clinging to the last string of connective tissue deep in my hip. I had a feeling it was sliding to a better place. It was a terrifying moment but also **not,** because—*You were the one asking me if I could do it.*

I felt old scar tissue breathing, then He said,

Do you remember, do you remember what happened here?

59

I replied, *"No… I honestly don't."*

He continued,

Shayla, he did some things to you that were absolutely horrific. Things that were directly intended to hurt me, through you. You were the victim. The VICTIM. I am going to empower you, through things other than just this. Things bigger than this.

Please do…

Thank You God, that sometimes there is no need for me to hear all of the details of the evil that was done to me. Thank You that You bring me only what I need. I trust You.

I plan to live a simple life here in America, then we'll go to Mexico.

Saturday April 7th 2018,

Dad sent Kelsey and I a text in the middle of the night that reads, "Can't sleep, truly love you two so much."

LIAR. IF YOU LOVED US YOU WOULDN'T BE DENYING THE TRUTH.

Dad, if what you feel for us is some broken version of love, I don't want your love. But you don't understand that do you?

My words are wasted. Part of me hopes that this case **does** make it to the courtroom so that way when I testify, you'll **have** to listen to me.

Monday April 9th 2018,

WOW, yeah... The pain in my body is gone. Prayer is EFFICIENT. *THANK YOU, JESUS.*

Friday April 13th 2018,

I have been having that fluttery butterfly feeling in my stomach lately...

It could be the Holy Spirit telling me something, or it could be a body-alert telling me that I have a lot going on. But I have had this much going on for a while now, so... I believe it's because something good is about to happen, something really good.

*God You've caused me to trust You by standing up to my father. You have matured me so that I now take what You say to heart. I listen and test what I "hear" you speak against Your **character** and Your **word**... Then I hold on tight to what is from You.*

I want us to talk right now.

*I know Your desire is for me to be **full** and energized by You. I would like some of that now, please.*

Tuesday April 17th 2018,

I went down to the altar for prayer like I do almost every Sunday (no shame in this healing game) and asked for prayer for my jaw, spine, and hip. One of my sisters (in Christ) laid her hand on my spine and the scoliosis pain was gone. She forgot to pray for my hip, but I know Jesus didn't forget. She asked that in Jesus' name all of my pain would be better, and that my jaw would actually be better than it ever was before, whatever that would look like. **And since then, I have been yawning like a normal person instead of restraining the width I open my mouth because of fear of it dislocating. AMEN.**

God asked me to smile after her prayers and I **barely** did. I was afraid of looking like a fool. I knew He wanted me to grin like a delighted child but I crumble-tofu-ed out (i.e. chickened out, it's 2018) and gave only a timid smile.

Ahh, help me be obedient in those moments. I want to be. I should be. Ah. Forgive me for caring so much about what others might think of me while I grin in delighted response to You. It's ridiculous to have any fear of this!

I still "feel" sensations in my jaw and spine, but I have faith that they are turning into memories that will no longer affect my body.

I can hardly wrap my brain around all of this. *Keep healing me, in all ways. Don't stop.*

God You're talking to me right now:

Sing Shayla
Dance Shayla
go downtown Shayla
be where you want Shayla
love me loudly Shayla

don't disappear on anyone Shayla

one more thing...

Trust me, with life, health and wealth. No worries. No space for them.

God, I believe that singing heals my jaw in a way that no other thing can. I believe that when I let out those notes it develops my voice for future singing projects, and when I do it, I use the power You've given me. I know You've created me to dance. I can't help but bump and twirl when music comes on. Thank You that this is something You want to do with me. Father, I do think that there is something in downtown Portland for me, it's unclear to me what it is but I feel a magnetic pull and I will yield to You. God, thank You for telling me to be where I want to be. This encourages me to use my voice, and to go for the good things You've put in my heart. YES, I will love You loudly! Help me so that I do not ditch relationships when things get tough and sticky. Help me trust You.

Saturday April 21st 2018,

Last night was the first night in my new place. I loved it.

Ah, it's a GIFT to not have to worry about waking baby Ronin or the dogs if I'm too loud getting ready in the morning.

I am so happy. I am so **blessed.** I've already cried a little since being here. **Life**—this world; SUCKS. And also; ROCKS.

If it weren't for everything happening how it happened; that car accident in 2015 messing me up so roughly, making me decide that I'd start living an obedient life to God, and then getting the settlement that gave me enough to live and focus

63

on this time of writing, singing, and healing, I would be in a different place. And I don't really care to know if that place would be better or worse, because I am here now. My desire for the wellbeing of others is expanding already. I am so excited to stay consistent in my creations. There is much good to be done on this earth by Shayla Danielle Laurendeau.

Tuesday May 1st 2018,

I put in my two weeks at EDGE today (the gym I teach yoga at).

In the email to my boss, I was going to say a bunch of fluffy stuff about offering to be a substitute and that I could be around if they're ever in a pinch, but that felt like disobedience. *That felt like doubting Your plan for this time. You've asked me to quit.* So, I typed out exactly what I needed to say.

Diana,

I love being at EDGE. I'm happy you emailed about this because I was going to reach out.

I am moving into downtown soon to put my head down and work on my writing and music. This is a big shift for me, I am taking it out of faith! We can speak more over the phone or in person about this if you'd like, but what that would look like is completely phasing myself out of EDGE. I know that was not the email you were expecting, nor was it what I had been planning. I do not want to leave abruptly, especially with all of the changes lately, but this is me stepping ALL IN to where I believe I need to be.

Shayla

My district manager emailed me prior to this asking me if I was happy with my schedule, and this is the reply she received. I currently teach 10 classes a week at this studio. That's a bit of a presence my manager's will have to fill. My prayer is that this does not give Diana a single gray hair, but rather, **hope** for new opportunities.

The old Shayla would have offered to phase out of the Happy Valley location and into the studio towards downtown. But that's not what God's been saying. He's been saying,

Quit.

He's been saying,

What do you think I want you to do?

And I've concluded that what He wants me to quit, removing all scheduled distractions so I can be all in to writing and music.

This is cray-cray God. This is me stepping out! I expect Your guidance, Your blessings, and Your strength. You've promised me all of this. You know why I am so sure of You? Because every word out of Your mouth is a promise. The only reason Your promises are ever broken is because of NOTHING. Never are they broken, even when I fail. You always have a blessing in the waiting. Even in times of straying. You are magnificent. This time is about YOU and me.

Recapping Your Magnificence

A while ago we had a quiet time together and You began whispering; asking if I was ready for a big career shift. With

everything in front of me, and knowing You know me, I concluded, "YES." I started to envision what You would lead me to. I know You know the deepest places in me so I thought, "Well, He's not taking me to work some desk-job so I can scratch anything like that off the list."

I know You want me to have rest from physical weariness.

I know also, that for a while You have been consistently whispering,

Sing for me Shayla.

So, it only makes sense for me to focus on that.

Father, when Jen's place came up for rent, I stopped asking You for guidance. I just went for it because it seemed like the most practical thing to do. It's a cute space, super close to work and I have a month-to-month lease so I can move out whenever I need. I took it upon myself to decide this decision made sense. You knew I was going to do that. Even though for some reason you wanted me at Brooklyn Yard. I love You. I will follow You until the end. The reality of me marching forward in faith and obeying You is that You could ask me to give up all of the money that I have received from the insurance settlement. We'll see. I believe You're calling me away from distractions into a place of submersion in You.

You had been asking me to go downtown, and for me to sing for you. So, I prayed, "God, I keep investing in ventures, ones that feel right and that sit heavy in my heart—and I don't want to do that anymore. I want to invest my time and resources where You want me to, and where I will abundantly grow and help others grow. So, if You truly want me to quit my job—overwhelm me with the notion."

And then You confirmed it through a woman at church. Cate. She randomly approached me during the service and asked if she could pray for me. And the rest of that story is for another day.

Friday May 4th 2018,

Yesterday my church community group met for the first time. It was sweet. We were all awkward and it was perfect. While we were eating our potluck smorgasbord I looked outside at Jan and Sylvia Weinstein's backyard. I had dreamt of their home before. I had already seen their backyard in my sleep, months ago. In my dream people were partying, and some of them were inviting me into the hot tub. I believe this happening was God's way of reminding me that He's in control. He has a plan, and it will always prevail. At the Weinstein's home, I felt the peace of God's sovereignty.

Yet even with the hope of God's plans unfolding, something does not feel good...

Life Scan

Dad is about to be arrested for the crimes he committed against me as a child. I didn't want this to happen. I thought we could deal with his discrepancies as a family; but he continues to deny ever abusing me. After approaching him directly first; then having trusted friends talk with him second, and the church dealing with him third, he's still not confessing... So, I felt it was my painful duty to report him to the police.

I also have sleep to catch up on.
I have been working a lot.
I am about to have no job.
I feel called to move downtown.
I need to sing for God, for Jesus.

I need to learn how to put music together.

Are any of these reasons to feel "off?" Life often has chaotic surprises, good and bad, this I know. So, what's with this dark feeling I am feeling?

Saturday May 5th 2018,

Happy Cinco de Mayo! I worked the front desk at EDGE today.

Boy did I feel **the resistance.**

The resistance: when God calls you to do something and the people around you give you nothing but reasons not to. Hearing of my leaving, many of my students cooed their, "No's."

But, NO. I will move to God's will.

Maybe they would be quieter if I told them specifically that God asked me to quit.

Faithfully trusting. That is what this journey is about. I am diving into an empty pool, praying there's water by the time I hit the bottom.

God this is me obeying. You are the light on this path. I will step out. I will be brave.

"Wisdom" means listening to You.

Shayla, we're going to do big things. Why do you think I have developed your appreciation for life? So you can help guide others. Work.

This will be work. Let me flow through you.
Don't cut the pipe off. Stay brave and bold my
little gentle soldier.

Thursday May 10th 2018,

Food. The devil is trying to attack me through food. I've not been able to control myself. I eat healthy foods, but SO much of it. I was looking and feeling good but then about a month ago I started to get tired and constantly sore, I think it's because I've been teaching so many heated fitness classes.

My "friend" when no other friend is around has always been food. I hate it and it's stopping **right now.** Most of us have a friend in food, but not like I have during the last few days. It's like a wild animal takes over my appetite when I'm past full. I'm addicted to the numbness of the multisensory moment. I remember as a child I used to sit and finish bags of chips or pretzels. My mom would get the big Costco bags and they wouldn't last long after I'd found them.

I started binge eating around the same time my dad finally left my body alone (the third grade). He "broke up" with me then, because of a mixture of things. It was dark outside. I was nine years old and lying on my bed as he told me that we had to stop our special relationship. Shortly before this talk, I had officially started my period, and because of that my mom gave me "the talk," to explain to me why my body was doing what it was. Because of all of this I'm sure my dad figured that his worlds would collide because I was getting old enough to connect the dots.

During my younger years, I lived two different lives. There was the life in the night, and the life in the day. They hardly touched one another. I was quiet and lived a full life in the daytime, with friends, church and soccer. And at night I stayed terrified. I was scared to go to bed and chronically paralyzed with fears that I didn't have the words to describe.

And now people around me tell me that I eat, "So healthy." But they don't see the way I sometimes use food when I need a friend. It's not okay. My heart beats fast and I let go of all of my self-control. My breath leaves my body and I rhythmically stuff myself because I can't find satisfaction. It's sad, it's quiet, and it's not okay.

God help me. I don't want to obsess over food like always. The only time I am able to stop obsessing about my weight is when I look good; when I can move and talk and not breathe weird or hate how I feel. My motivation is to permanently be in that state of balanced bliss where the feeling of my physical body does not hold me back from participating in life.

Why do I go into animal mode after I am past full?

It's the only legal, widely accepted vice that drowns everything out for a second.

Wild Animal
A Poem by Shayla Danielle Laurendeau

All the chaos
all the anxious thoughts and moments
everything that has happened

everything that will happen

everything that I've done
and everything that's been done to me.

Poof.

One moment of me, silencing it all.

I ache for more moments where I can **wildly be.** After everything in my life, I am this woman right now who takes life too seriously.

I am a woman who cannot laugh at herself, I don't want to mess up.

I don't want to say "Oops, hehehe."

There is wisdom in wanting to operate efficiently and successfully, but why can't I couple this with laughter?

I'm leaving for Florida soon to visit my girl Rosa Reyna. I used to be her barista, and then her and I worked together at a salon and our friendship blossomed. Something's always drawn me to her. She's gorgeous, strong, opinionated (in a good way) and quiet at the same time. She's not one who's quick to befriend people, I like that about her. She's careful about the people she lets in her life. She permanently pursues educating herself, and she pays attention to her body's telling signs and moves her life accordingly.

Thank You for beautiful Rosa.

Wednesday May 16th 2018,

Thank You for this staycation. Today was supposed to be my second day in Florida, but it's stormy there all week so I cancelled my plans until there's sunshine when I go.

Now this weekend I get to go to the dream workshop at Church... YAY.

You speak to me through dreams... I believe it's because that's when we're most spiritually "awake." Our loud predispositions fall asleep so You're not at war with our small-minded human thoughts.

Dream

When I was younger, I had this recurring dream of a larger-than-me ladybug chasing and chasing me. The dream always ended with her capturing me on my bed... I sometimes even felt the pressure of her weight on me.

Interpretation

My dad was this ladybug. Ladybugs are harmless. Even when they're large. He did chase me and chase me, and in the moments when I was crushed, I was crushed. But the aftermath of those times that he "captured me" is simply this:

I am healed.

I am whole.

I am clean.

These realities are now as harmless as the touch of a ladybug.

Now I have more detailed dreams, and they continue to mean things.

GET OUT OF YOUR FLESH you SINNERS (myself included). I'm tired of humanity, **so** tired. I want to lock myself in a jungle with no technology except for a laptop that only lets me write books.

I want a permanent reprieve. Heaven?

I desire someone to laugh with.

I am called to live a bright life, abundantly, with a calling bigger than I can see. Bigger than any single
moment
I
will
ever   have.

I am called to live for the one moment You gave me.

The death of Your flesh, on that cross.

I have faith for the story You've written for me. I have faith that as I do it Your way my heart will never have ever been so full.

A new slate, with Your guidance is what I believe I am saying yes to.

You know what else I believe I am saying yes to? Something **bigger** than what I can imagine.

You call Your children to dream dreams bigger than they can handle on their own, that way they have to depend on You.

That's the kind of dream I want to hold.

```
I would want my life to end if it wasn't
for the fact that God is working out
everything that I have for the better.
```

Life sucks. There is too much to it and I just want to be home, in heaven.

I don't feel like asking for it, but I need to. I need help. I need help seeing the purpose behind every breath. Sometimes things "click," and I feel purposed, and other times I'm rattled with aimlessness.

I AM SO TIRED OF PEOPLE and the way they faithlessly function through life.

Like I do.

I am finding what is least appealing about myself through each of my frustrations...

I dislike:

1. People worrying about mundane things.
2. People talking about mundane things.
3. Mundane things.

Right now, my eyes only see only what irritates me.

I do see the influence of God's people slowly taking over my rhythms...

I see them living out what You say to.

Most Sundays someone from the congregation tells us about the work the church has been doing for the community, or in what way they themselves have benefitted from the church's support. *It's good to see Your fruit.*

And even without the declarations of fruitfulness in church I still encounter the goodness of your children during daily interactions and conversations.

Help me, I am desperate now.

Shayla, calm down. What are you running from as you eat more than you should and as you numb out your mind with Netflix?

I'm running from... Life. From hating life.

I'm running from You.

Every time I numb out it's my life-pause button.

I am not *the one with the controller. Or rather, I shouldn't be. I would pause for life. Thank You that Your will and purposes are better than mine. I want to want what You want, because truly, You love me more than I love myself. So, don't let me want anything that You don't want. Make my will match Yours. The truth is: You've given me the strength to exercise self-control. End of story. No thing before me will ever be too much that You haven't given me a way out of temptation. You've promised this.*

"No temptation has overtaken you except what is common to mankind. And God is faithful; he will not let you be tempted beyond what you can bear. But when you are tempted, he will also provide a way out so that you can endure it."

1 Corinthians 10:13 NIV

It's easier when you're numb. It's easier when you're not working or doing. Just, numbing. Nothing happens, nothing changes.

I am running from risks. I am running from faith in where I know I'll go.

I am running from healing. What happens when I am unstoppable? What will be expected of every waking moment? What kind of people will I be mashed up with? The most amazing, I'm sure.

What kind of things will I have to say as I exhort people? What kind of life will I have?

I imagine a life that is challenging in all of the right places.

I have already been tortured before, in every zone a human being could be (body, mind and spirit). So what am I afraid of?

I am fearful now of the opposite… Of success through Christ.

Thursday May 24th 2018,

Today's coffee date with my coworker and fellow yogi Frances Brower was a quick answer to my prayer of encountering more of You in people. As our coffee date commenced, she expressed she wanted to connect with me because she's also wanting to enjoy more of You through people.

It's funny, I'm becoming one of those cheesy Jesus-girls I used to be royally put-off by.

- I never want to be unapproachable because of my faith
- I want to be humble and cheesy in HIM
- I'm down [just] SO DOWN with Jesus though

Last night I wanted to smoke weed. My lower back was hurting, and it sounded like a nice way to say goodbye to pain. I didn't end up smoking so ten points for me.

Saturday May 26th 2018,

Yesterday.

I don't know how to describe it, but I'll try…

The grand jury was at 9AM. (A grand jury is a collection of people who are given jury duty and then vote for validity (evaluate the accusations) so that the case does or doesn't go to the courtroom. My mom, our family pastor and I showed up to testify. Kelsey was there for moral support.

There were a few people escorting us through the process, lots of law jargon then all of a sudden it was time to testify. The District Attorney was generous in the way he described to me how things would go. He told me he'd have to ask me intimate questions in front of these people and that I'd have to answer.

I don't know if it was the fluorescent lights or the white details in the room that made me feel strange. I felt cold inside. All of the people who sat around that table looked at me like I was a little girl. I was the youngest in the room, but people don't normally look at me the way those strangers did. And none of them nodded their heads in condolence when I confessed what my dad did to me. There was an emptiness surrounding me. I felt naked as I described to them the abuse I received when I was young. I barely looked around at their faces. I'm a person's person; connecting with the room comes naturally to me, but those strangers who looked at me like I was little could hardly look at me, so I stopped looking at them. There was one juror in particular that seemed to have an opinion about me before I walked into the room. It looked like she had already announced something to the room. It looked like she had already declared herself as leader of the jurors. The rest of them seemed to silently bow to her power. Then my part was over, and because it was the last day that that batch of jurors was called to duty, we ran out of time for them to make a verdict. That means that we're going to start over, with a new batch of jurors. So, that first batch of strangers heard my story for only God knows why. My guess is it's because they needed to hear what God had to tell them through my testimony.

Wednesday June 6th 2018,

When you're alone on a Wednesday evening at McMenamin's; writing and sitting cross-legged in shorts for 20 minutes and you switch the cross of your legs, you have a very humbling experience while peeling them off of the vinyl seat.

Sunday June 10th 2018,

A woman who prayed over me this evening said she was getting the sense of You speaking "Jewelry" over me, that I will create jewelry, "And people will look at the pieces and know the hand of God made them."

This is throwing me for a loop.

God, I haven't heard You say anything about creating jewelry?

What if it's a metaphor of what I'll create? Of what I'll adorn His creations with?

Hmm.

Sunday June 17th 2018,

Tonight, at church, I went down to the altar for prayer. It's Father's Day, and they called down those who wanted prayer because of broken relationships with their fathers. Whoa. A woman prophesied that what I will do will involve foster children, girls and tiaras.

God instructed me to hold on to her words.

Hmm.

Monday June 25th 2018,

Uhm, uhm, uhm, the first grand jury was hard.

And how odd is it that we're doing it again because we ran out of time the first time?

I've already lost any steam I had to write about it.

Tuesday June 26th 2018,

I woke up at 7AM after not sleeping much last night. *We processed, processed, processed.* I was hungry all night while my gut digested unprocessed information resting in my body.

I was too tired to feed myself, so I lay awake, an observer to my body's fantastic way of being. It felt like the files inside of me were being sorted.

And now today I feel the most amazing I could ever feel. I am energized physically, mentally and spiritually. My body looks great, my eyes are not puffy, and I'm ready to go.

The second grand jury is at 1:15PM today.

I know I have armies praying for me.

Thank You for life. XO.

Friday July 20th 2018,

It's crazy that we spend so much of our life healing from the brokenness that we were born into.

I cannot wait for the day where no healing work will need to be done.

For now: GROWTH; COMMENCE.

And in the meanwhile, Father, let me peacefully understand that I don't understand You fully.

Monday July 23rd 2018,

A while ago God said to me,

Are you ready to quit your job?

And although the prompt sent my head into a wild frenzy, I couldn't shake the idea. I had the impression that He was asking a loaded question, one where He was also asking if I was ready to spend more time pursuing singing. I told Him, *"If that's what you want me to do, then You have to confirm it. You have to make someone at church confirm that You're asking me to quit my job, **without** me having to go down to the altar for prayer."* And the next Sunday I was at church and a random woman approached me, saying, "God has asked you to do something."

I shattered, in the best way.

That's when I decided I would step into this trust fall. *I believe in whatever You have planned for me.* I believe.

I was given a lot of money from an insurance settlement after a man, driving drunk, hit me in a head-on collision in 2015. I was physically broken for a few years. I was on pain meds, muscle relaxers, weed and sleeping pills. I spent a lot of time with chiropractors, massage therapists, and my acupuncturist. And throughout that time, I knew that I would receive some sort of insurance settlement for my pain, but I didn't know how much. I mused through the ideas of buying a business or going to school. But when the money came, I started renting my own place and shortly after that's when God started to speak to my heart; asking me if I was ready to quit my job. I was terrified. The idea felt so against-the-grain. The practical thing would have been to build something with my money and my time. The wise thing would have been to invest my money in a sure return. I did get my 200-Hour Yoga Teaching Certification during that time, and that worked out very well for me. But we mostly invested time here. In these pages. And I see that now. The Healing Diary was the thing I built with God with that money. And my studio album was birthed during that time, during long uninterrupted nights of talking, crying, and worshipping. I had many sleepless nights there, wide awake, writing, singing, and recording new melodies. With God's whispers I wrote music.

No.

He'd say to lyrics.

Yes.

He'd say to others.

I've learned to yield to His will, creatively. He's faithful to guide me. He's faithful to show up as my father. Our partnership is hard. Sometimes I love something I write or record and He says, "No," so I get rid of it. Other times I don't want to write something that He asks me to, but I obey. When these moments happen a piece of me dies and another comes to life. My stomach gets frustrated but then I'm delighted when I see the fruit of His prompt. In this same co-creative way, we've deleted my will and left His will in this book. I'm not perfect at it, my skills are growing just like they would in any field of work, but He is the best teacher, and I want His fingerprints all over my work more than I want mine.

Wednesday July 25th 2018,

It's nice to think about today being the first day of the rest of my life. Thinking with this perspective makes me feel like there's a clean slate of possibility ahead of me.

I can only try to imagine the future. It **has to be** significant, otherwise I do not understand what life is.

Flower Blossom
A poem by Shayla Laurendeau

To glow completely as one's self
radiating full blossom of the harvest that is your life

is a choice to brace the head on wind
of society's false presumption

that misery can always find company.

Look to the dying bulbs on the right; left, and absolutely
behind.

Shake the weeds, you will, when morning's light reveals your
perpetually vibrant petals.

It's beautiful to feel freedom from chains that previously bound me.

Perfectionism is lost, and far away from the home it had in me.

God has his hands out, palms up saying "Child, drop them here. Your worries, your pain, your ridiculous anxieties.

Listen to me nudge you. Watch what I have made you good at. Long for what I have made you great at. Your gifts **glow,** my power is in you. It is DONE."

Saturday July 28th 2018,

I felt gross this morning. My body felt fine (by my happy surprise) but my heart felt gross.

I recently hung out with a once upon a time close friend. I have intentionally pulled away from her. I don't want to engage with life like her and I used to. It wasn't healthy.

Now I stand like a deer in headlights wondering, *How do I navigate this still-cherished connection?*

While I was broken and miserable after the accident in 2015, I decided I wanted to live a straighter life. I was ready to stop resisting the truth.

A few things I was certain of:
1. It was time to stop doing illegal things, so the MDMA I did every few occasions **had** to go.
2. Sex is to be saved for the sacred, special bond of marriage, so no more of that until my wedding day.
3. Lying to my parents about where I was staying the night at, when really, I was staying at my boyfriend's, needed to stop.

These three things were the most obvious. They never sat in my body well. And it actually felt great to stay within these boundaries.

Boundaries. Let's talk about 'em.

After I made this short list of boundaries, I started having a **terribly tough** time making **any** decision. I was keeping receipts way more than usual just in case I wanted to take purchases back, and I was spending hours at the grocery store choosing between very few items. After this odd indecisiveness my therapist prompted me to name my boundaries. He said because I didn't have defined boundaries my decisions were getting blurry. So, I worked out what I believe and how that should affect my choices, and I chose more boundaries.

And after working those out I felt free. So now, I am going to find boundaries for my friendships too.

I am well educated on who I want to be **and am** right now. But **without fail** you can find me standing around with some less-than-impressive characters. It's not uncommon for you to find me around a drug dealer or at a party where I am not sure if **any** conversation is worth having because most people are past memory retention ability.

Why do I wander into these spaces?

How do I wander into these spaces?

How to Choose Friendships

My Values	My Boundaries	My Choices
Living a life that glorifies God.

Enjoying life.

Loving well. | Doing illegal things.

Gossip.

Staying stagnant in life. | Lay each new friendship before Yahweh.

Being clear with people on why I won't come and hang out. |

Wednesday August 1st 2018,

Hello diary. I write to you today from my spot on the floor. I'm leaning back on the wall, gazing at the only plant I own in its moldy soil. Should I be embarrassed to want success in my ventures? Absolutely not. Should I feel guilty if I desire it for my own glory? Yes. What legacy of mine lasts if I work only for myself?

Sunday August 5th 2018,

My friend, Calico Skadungeh!

Thank you for gracing me with your presence here in Portland yesterday. I'm so happy Rosa introduced us in Florida. You are an intentional dude. I can tell you have lived. You live in this world with as much ease as you have.

I'm thankful for the dynamic of our friendship. As I was walking around this morning talking with God (like I shared with you I do) I was describing to Him our kind of communication. I was telling Him how when you ask me your million-dollar questions, I am so peaceful when answering them because I never see a flicker of judgement take over your face. You create a space that gives others complete expressive permission. I can fearlessly share all that I'd like to say, that's a huge deal.

Thank you for winging-it while hanging out with me. The night began with me forgetting my wallet at home, and you teaching me to be chill about it. Then later we were let into a Timbers game for free (after you convinced the kid working the gate to let us in). Winging it is a blast.

One of the million-dollar questions you asked me was, "What are those weird things you do that no one would really think that Shayla would do?" And I gave you a couple answers, but now that I've had time to think about it, I've figured out a better one.

I lie.

I catch myself giving people **typical** answers to the questions they ask, out of my desire not to be vulnerable. I tell people, "Yeah sure, I'd love to come," when I would much rather stay at home. I tell people, "I'm **fine,**" when really, I want the world to **shut down** but don't want to talk about it. I stay quiet in situations where I should be righteously flipping tables. That feels like lying to me. And oftentimes I laugh with people as they do something they shouldn't do because I don't want to be fiercely Christlike and correct them how I know I should.

And because of these lies I am in last year's emotions, wrapped up under cheap saran wrap, barely staying contained.

Best,
Shayla Danielle Laurendeau

Friday August 6th 2018,

Hello, I write to you today from the top of the tall dining room table that Jen left me when she moved out of this place. Sitting up here gives me a perspective that feels brighter and higher than my usual view. I am able to ditch all of my duties below and see this time as marked for things bigger than the usual.

This evening I started to watch a movie but then I realized that I still had some antsy energy in me. I knew that I had to create something before the day was done. Like Jack and the Beanstalk, I found my way up here for intellect's zone switch.

Into creation mode I rolled. I recorded two songs, only voice (as usual). And boy, did these songs have me in a **zone.** I feel more Shayla-expression flowing with each passing day.

And boom! Boom! Boom! I crossed things off of the soul list today! I made some tough phone calls that should have been made A WHILE ago. And you know what gave me the strength?

Talking it out, out loud to You, Our Creator. Giving You my fears for the worst outcome, and then laughing with myself about the low-level irrelevance of the worst-case scenarios.

Thank You for gracing me with strength today. Can I have more?

Sunday August 8th 2018,

I just cooked myself the YUMMIEST lunch. I'll call it a: deconstructed tofu-veggie-quinoa roll. AH. So good. I cooked the quinoa, chopped some veggies, sauteed tofu in some ginger, then threw coconut aminos and sriracha on top.

My limbs feel limp. I definitely got enough sleep last night, so the aspiring doctor in me is drawing health questions out of the wellness file in my brain. Maybe the emptying conversation I had with my dad last night has me worn. It was 10:36PM when I was finished talking to him. It felt much later than that, so I crawled into bed with my body's finished feeling. It was the longest time I have been able to speak to him without him treating me poorly. There was no laughing at me while I shared my heart's fullest expression. It was the first time I have been able to say the absolute truth to him after a disagreement. It was the first time I had no qualm to whether or not he heard, empathized, or listened.

As I sat alone in my home on my spot on the floor, I imagined God taking my dialogue to my dad in his jail cell. I even tried to picture his face through a textured section on the ceiling I was locking eyes with. I unloaded **all** of it. I forgave my dad for everything he's done, everything he might do, and everything he will not be.

Monday August 9th 2018,

Music... I can't stop writing it. What kind of vibe do I want to give people?

Do I want to save people with sound, like Justin Bieber's music does? Or do I want to pull them into their soul? Or am I dying to do **both?** I write melodic ponders and good stories to fill this earth with. And so far, I have enough songs to make a few albums. The lyrics keep coming to me, so I keep recording them in voice notes and on pieces of paper. I write about being careful with your heart, abstinence, racism, heaven, the fact that my dad took my virginity, strippers, the night I remembered that my dad abused me, being infectiously joyful, human love, and being thirsty for God's love. You'll see. These songs are truly for the ones that God gets them to.

I am so excited to join the Apprentice Cohort at church! (A discipleship program.) **AH**. *You're going to do **things** through this! I can't wait. I ask and pray now that I am energized to step out, and that this cohort brings my needed music collaborators together. I feel more and more Your desire for me to live closer to downtown for You. Something is going to happen. Something good. I will be ready.*

You gave me a vision today. You asked me to stand up and hold out my hands.

I did then I was holding a large ice cube with a piece of thin brown paper on top of it. I was standing in the forest, in the snow.

You're peeling the paper off of the top of my glassy ice cube to display it to the world. I believe this vision you gave me today resembles an icy, time-sensitive art I am to share with the world.

That's really cool... I broke down the vision on a piece of paper.

Cubes; three-dimensional, different sides, complete, whole, full...

Ice; time sensitive, fragile, pure, cooling, transparent, holographic...

Brown Wrapping Paper; calm, resourceful wrapping...

Snow; there are only specific seasons and places where snow happens...

Forest; calm, restorative, like-minded with God, being in the nature of things...

This is about music, my love. What's more three-dimensional than sound?

Friday August 10th 2018,

Life is good, I went to Rachel Jacquin's today. It felt like hanging out with a sister, because that's what she is.

Saturday August 11th 2018,

Our time always comes with clarity and peace.

Today, I was reminiscing about a time in high school when my friend and I were sharing some codeine cough syrup while we were in ceramic class. I had snuck the liquid in from my family's medicine collection at home. Dad would get these terrible coughs, and this particular time he was really sick with them (hence the codeine in the cough syrup).

Anyways, I received a "C" in sculpting. I didn't make a single project in that class. Thank goodness my friend did and thank goodness she made some good ones because I think our teacher would have defended my grade to any teacher-police by counting my assistance to her.

Younger me didn't have the capacity to deal with everything I endured, so I did what I did. Even in my stupidity You cover me. Why have You chosen me to love so much? I don't want to test Your love. I desire to give You no reason to hold your favor away from me.

God's watched me and protected me, and believe me, He's also dealt with me.

Wednesday August 15th 2018,

It's 10:20AM. My coffee date at Singer Hill with Frances Brower just wrapped up.

You are a breath of **fresh air,** girl.

Frances told me about her mission work in Alaska. She told me about serving hotdogs to the fishermen, and about Brenda Crim. Brenda Crim is a woman whose heart is for Jesus. Her team at Alaska Missions & Retreats provides food and childcare along an Alaskan shore for fishermen (they do this and many other things). They are simply there to meet a need. Their mission is: "Transforming hearts and lives with the message of hope in Christ."

Frances told me about how Alaska was brutally wounded by people coming to Alaska and sexually abusing children. Now Alaska Missions & Retreats is doing a big part in helping to break that narrative by loving people well. Brenda runs teams to help people get "unstuck" from tough places they've fallen into. Her teams bless the area in a way that unwinds the damaging narratives that have come before.

God would You please heal this land in a way that I know You can. Fully and with loud love.

Thursday August 16th 2018,

Sugar is poison. The anger I feel today is from a sugar craving.

I'm dog sitting this weekend... I said yes to helping Rachel because I want to **show up** for her, even if watching her dog (or any dog) isn't usually my cup of tea.

I thank You for the outlet that is our creative creations. I thank You for the wine I am drinking that I have faith I have inherited the ability to create from water.

I just lifted up my water in prayer and it's still water. That's fine, I still believe.

Friday August 17th 2018,

YES. I'm sitting at Pete's Coffee and it's only 9:33AM. I'm winning.

I feel down though.

Dream

Last night I had a dream that I was out partying with friends. It was a holiday. It was the type of scene where you felt like you were on a TV set. Everyone glowed an abundant level of charisma, even though I only spoke to a few. In my heart I knew we were in Taiwan. **Taiwan is a specific symbol**

because in America so many things are made in Taiwan. Then, people started to drink. We all swirled around through darkness and intoxication began slipping over my body.

This dream set my head into a weird space for the day, it made me feel guilty for living in the typical, and for getting drunk in this dream even when I didn't in reality.

Interpretation

This dream wasn't from You. You don't deposit dreams into my psyche so that I feel bad about myself.

"In peace I will both lie down and sleep; for you alone, O LORD, make me dwell in safety."

Psalm 4:8 ESV

Dreams like the one I had last night are only allowed to happen to me so that the Lord can instruct me. And in this case, I am being taught not to let the enemy have his way with my mood for accusing me of something I didn't do.

Note

Thank you Community Group (church small group),

For not asking about my dad. Thank you for not asking about what happened after I testified at the grand juries. I don't know what to say or how to feel, or how I want to be treated or not treated. I am too busy suffocating myself with distractions right now.

Shayla

Saturday August 19th 2018,

I want **practical** things to work on to help my studio album's completion. There is an **overflow** of melodic lyricism that flows out of me, but I am barely functional to move past this creation phase.

What's my next move?

I thank You that I didn't just drown myself in the internet, googling: "What does a singer-songwriter musician need to do to have a career?"

I will work on what I can.

The one thing I am sure of that bridges the gap between the big questions and the big answers is: faith. I **believe.**

To have faith is to believe. To have faith is to **march on,** learning and clinging to what I can and letting myself stay content in the unknown.

Wednesday August 22nd 2018,

Today's conscious moments began at 4AM and now at 3PM I feel like I could simultaneously lay down for bed and jump out of my body at the same time.

Reality
A poem by Shayla Danielle Laurendeau

At 4AM I was abruptly woken.

Shortly after,

something felt different about my life.

Something felt different about me.

I believe (I have goosebumps writing this now) that at 4AM on this full August day God anointed me with fearlessness.

I have concluded it was fearlessness because at 4AM my precious REM cycle was disturbed by the most demonic cat screech I have ever heard. It came from just outside my bedroom window. I believe God allowed this cat to be assigned to the task of terrifying me because He knew of the outcome.

God **knew** that after the rounds of screeching I would be **immediately** charged with a fire to **burn brighter.**

When I woke, I was frightened and then immediately disgusted by the situation. I knew it wasn't from God but rather a test He allowed to strengthen me.

satan's attempts at shattering my peace will only create a deeper passion in me to spread Jesus' peace over myself and every soul under heaven.

You see that satan? satan's attempts at shattering my peace will only create a deeper passion in me to spread Jesus' peace over myself and every soul under heaven.

Thursday August 23rd 2018,

My refrigerator light is out and has been out for a while… I don't think refrigerators should have lights anyways, we probably shouldn't eat in the dark.

***Thank You** for today's 3AM **gentle** wake up call. I rose from my bed, turned my soft lights on, laid back down, and You spoke to my heart.*

The devil plants evil seeds regularly enough in peoples' lives to cause them to create space in themselves for demons to influence them deeply enough for them to torment a little girl.

"Submit yourselves, then, to God. Resist the devil, and he will flee from you." James 4:7 NIV

I want to expect the best. I want to expect the **most my trust** with God can handle at any given moment.

My senses feel heightened right now. Eyesight, heart space and faith are flowing so **freely** around me. *Thank You for keeping my eyes open throughout the growth of my abilities. I want to see. I want to see it all. It's freaky, really.*

Truth feels good to speak. Speaking the truth takes the equivalent weight off of a being as the dead weight of another's body (I assume).

Dream

I had a dream of a woman covered in sparkles last night. It was awesome (sparkles always make me happy). In the dream I knew that she was glittery because she had had a connection with me. We were at some sort of red-carpet event and people kept noticing her sparkles and they traced it back to me, gleefully. She fondly and frequently gazed my way as I admired the aftermath of our time together. This was a beautiful dream.

Interpretation

I believe this woman represents the things I am creating. Specifically, I believe she represents the movies that will be created from my writings. I think this woman was the woman who plays the main character, me. She is covered in glitter because she is the glowing version of me. She plays the bright version that I want to show the world I've become because of God. She's the authentic me that did the healing work so that she could go out and glow.

I believe this dream was a beautiful message from God that speaks to me: "Keep going, woman."

Also, I specifically asked God for a glittery dream before bed last night. Lately satan has been using dreams to attack my energy for the day. Not today! AMEN.

It's my baby sister's birthday today. I can't wait to see the beauty that continues to unfold in her life. Her existence is a gift to me.

Sunday August 26th 2018,

I wrote a song this morning called, *Oh, my God.*

Oh My God

Oh, my God
Oh my God
Oh my God
Oh my God
Your holiness blows me away
Your faithfulness is
Your faithfulness
It gets me it gets me it gets me
Your holiness gives to me (gives to me gives to me)

God is my refuge and strength
Always ready to help in times of trouble
Oh, my God
Oh, my God
Oh, my God

Please
Please don't stop lo-vin' me
Oh, my God

Its inspiration came from a ridiculously joyful moment where I felt totally loved.

I saw (in my heart) a picture of complete healing over my life. I had a feeling of shamelessness about the truth of Christ, and felt no wound holding me back.

You can literally see the bright emotions on my face as you listen to the recording.

Thursday August 30th 2018,

During our 2:30AM healing time yesterday we scanned my body head-to-toe and You asked me why different parts of my body hurt. While doing this I discovered that one of my dispositions is that: I act like I am the most important person in the world...

Just before that revelation I was boiling some water for coffee and my insanely loud smoke detector went off because a piece of food caught on fire under the stovetop burner. This jolted my senses into a state of fearful and ready vulnerability. It helped me get honest about things that I have not been able to. The noise-assault left me desperate for healing.

Early yesterday morning, I was able to release memories that were keeping my body locked. I confessed lies that were spoken over me and I told God the not-yet-said abusive acts that my father committed against me.

Jesus spoke something sweet over every piece of my body as He told me to let go of what I remembered.

This was a lengthy healing session and for a moment it felt unnecessary, but for some reason we didn't stop. I viscerally reacted to what He spoke over me, finding myself twisting and unwinding from shapes associated with the memories. We moved through every inch of me and afterwards I felt undeservingly purified.

You deserve to be clean.

My day continued in a wonder… This was an experience like none I've had. And later, I talked to dad again.

```
Alone in my home, I imagined God taking
my words to my dad's jail cell.
```

I told him I loved him and that I don't think he's disgusting. I told him that I think I will see him in heaven.

"If you openly declare that Jesus is Lord and believe in your heart that God raised him from the dead, you will be saved. For it is by believing in your heart that you are made right with God, and it is by openly declaring your faith that you are saved." Romans 10:9-10 NLT

That is all you have to do to be saved. That is all you have to do to have everlasting life. My dad did Romans 10:9-10. He openly declared that Jesus is Lord, and from what I could tell he believed in his heart that God raised Jesus from the dead. So, I believe that after all my dad's done, I'll still see him in eternity.

I want to detach any security I might have in an identity that could become glorified because of living life with mass exposure.

I think I know what it would be like to be a vastly known human, but I am sure you just **don't know** until you know.

I believe my dream of the glittery woman was God showing me that I will indeed be able to distinguish the difference between myself and the divinely given gifts **He** has put in me to share for **His** glowing success in this world.

AMEN.

God, please do the work needed in me so that I can healthily perform… So that I can healthily sing… So that I can healthily engage in relationships… And so that I can abundantly enjoy life.

After I do slow meditation breaths and/or workout really hard my face tingles. It must be the feeling of blood flowing freely through my face. I love letting it sit and do its thing. It's a moment when I seem to get a full, easy breath into my body.

The craziest patience I exercise letting those inhales slowly enter my body after pressing every sip of air out.

Sunday September 2nd 2018,

Yesterday, mom said: "You know Lauren Dai…?"

Me: "Daigle? Yes."

Mom: "I think your voice sounds like her."

Me: "Wow that's cool that you say that because I practice singing her songs a lot, wow that's funny you say that." [While internally I was saying] "Oh my gosh that comment will encourage me for a long while to believe that something of anything can come from me singing."

I had mom over to make vegan, gluten-free pancakes and they ended up being more of a crumble-situation. In my defense, cast iron pans are very hard to pancake with. Those crumbles were yummy though. So was spending time with mom.

Honey
A Poem by Shayla Danielle Laurendeau

Yesterday evening I lie with my back on the hard floor.

With the ceiling high above me I listened to You.

My home is hollow enough for You to fill with Your presence.

We did work in this quiet place.

I wanted to stop a few times, I felt like I pushed enough.

"Keep going," You said… So I did until I sobbed.

Monday September 3rd 2018,

DID YOU KNOW that orange wine is a thing? Wow and amen for Shalom Y'all Israeli Street Food.

I had dinner with Christa (a friend from Bridgetown) last night. We had a good time building each other up. After dinner we walked to church and were getting ready to serve on the welcoming team, and she asked me if I was okay. I told her I have a hard relationship with my dad, and that right now it's beating me down. She let me know I don't have to always be "okay" with her, and that I can bring the whole me. She then prayed with me. *Jesus, I am thankful for YOU.* AH. *Thank You that Christa saw me.*

It's a hard process, this forgiveness stuff. Nausea washes over my body as I recall a young, helpless me.

I feel like I have forgiven him… I have.

I forgive him.
He did terrible things to me.
He let demons take over his body because he wouldn't deal with them himself.
Then the demons would crawl their way into my room.

I did talk with that cute coffee boy from New Seasons again this evening. *Ha-ha, thank you Jesus for the blueberry craving that drove me to the store.*

Wednesday September 5th 2018,

What a lovely coffee date with Cate Mccoy…. *God You are so encouraging.* I am so happy Cate and I met. I was able to encourage her and she did the same for me. *It was beautiful to bounce back and forth in Your spirit with one another. I feel so heightened and filled by You. Thank You for Cate and thank You for our fun chatter.*

When God asked me if I was ready to quit my job and I told him He'd have to confirm it by bringing someone to me, **Cate was the woman who randomly approached me to tell me that God had asked me to do something.**

Your higher understanding will always be better and more than my own. Continue to constantly deposit Your wisdom in me.

Dream

Last night I dreamt that I was that in a grocery store pouring my coffee like I do when I go to New Seasons. As I poured the coffee it was down to its last bit and it started to get moldy, so I looked towards coffee boy to have him fix it and saw that he was chopping a huge block of uncooked meat. I thought this was weird because he was in the coffee-making zone. Then, a man walked up to me and poured himself some coffee from the next pot. I looked past him at coffee boy while this closer man began chattering about his recent shift to veganism for his health. "My Doctor has me trying it." He stated. I tried to engage with this closer man as much as I could, but I selfishly did it out of hopes to get coffee boy to longingly look my way. Then me and vegan man turned to the left to see a dark range rover gently t-boning a green jeep in the parking lot... There was some chatter that went like, "Well, that's what they have been told their cars are for." And after the crash it seemed as though the jeep could no longer function even though it appeared to have extremely minimal damage.

Holy Spirit, fill me, in Your way... Let me know if it makes sense to receive the message of this dream now or if we should sit down and draw it out later...

Now it is.

Interpretation

*You don't want me to look past who and what goodness, **cohesive goodness** You're bringing into my life. This coffee boy is into things that don't vibe with me, and some of what he produces is toxic. Uhg... God, I receive... Let me receive as much as I need to. Open my heart... I want to see past niceness and sweet vibes and charm. I want to believe this is not a call to halt noticing coffee boy, but a filling of your discernment. Show me if it means deeper. You are AMAZING. You filled me in my sleep to show me the realities of what his story is. Let me be brave to **boldly** guard my heart and "X" him out of any love story of mine if need be. I want to bravely and boldly take Your wisdom into my functioning self. I will follow You on this patient walk to spiritual abundance, where I seek satiation in Your word and from Your spirit. Goodness will be the vibe* *from my future husband. You have made me a spiritually hungry woman who is and will not be satisfied by the simple kindnesses of this earth. Make my heart want Your highest gifts. I will not shoulder the burden of the heavy-yoke-walk with an unbelieving lover. Bar too high? Never with You. Like Bethany Allen taught us on Sunday at Bridgetown… Jesus will **never** be put in a box. Never. Let my heart and whole being be open to seeing You.*

I still have hopes for this coffee boy.

I don't know if it's silly, or if I can say that a life with Jesus means that the Holy Spirit informs me so that I can know how to pray so that what the enemy desires to be a weed can turn into a flower's blossom.

God You give me life. Plant the seeds for the beautiful harvest of our life. Let every breath, every walk, every conversation be a picture of You. Glow glow glow. Into me, out of me and around me. This little light of mine.

Thursday September 6th 2018,

Hey.

Today was the day we were supposed to go to court.

We didn't.

Dad's lawyer asked for the date to be pushed back because she wasn't done interviewing her witnesses, whatever that means.

Blah blah blah. I could describe to you the worry that wants to eat my family, or I could tell you about the empty feeling in the new place for love in my heart, or—I could describe to you the truest state of my being which is: hopeful in every way for God to delegate, direct and provide.

God, I dare You to do more with me than I could dream.

Growing, it hurts. It sucks really.

Dream

I had a dream last night that a man came into my home and tried to rape me. He was big and I was fighting as best as I could, so I did the move I knew how to best and I slid my hand down his pants and snapped his penis in half. His whole body fell. I wasn't done. I bent it in every which way my strength and time would allow, and he didn't fight back with one inch of his body.

I don't know how to say this—so I won't, I'll type it. **I'm not afraid of life, I'm not afraid of death. I'm not afraid of loneliness, boredom, of over exertion or blessed abundance.**

I'm afraid of failing. Not in a career or any relational way. I'm afraid of **not getting it.** I stand at the center of a teeter totter balancing between doing work for the Lord and resting in the meek abilities of my humanness.

Help me.

Friday September 7th 2018,

I had a wonderful morning with my friend Sylvia Weinstein. We had coffee at her home. It was really nice getting to know her and her sweetness. She calls herself a simple person who loves to cook, take care of her home and the people God brings into her life. She's the definition of a great woman.

It was encouraging to chat with Jan (Sylvia's husband) about what he's reading… I liked that he called me a thinker when I told him why the books he's reading interest me. It was nice that anxieties about my jaw causing me pain didn't haunt me during our conversation. Jan knows how to talk the good talk we all need to hear. I'm happy in this world there are people with the stamina to teach until listeners reach maximum learning capacity… We all need more truth.

*Father, make the good teachers **louder**.*

Saturday September 8th 2018,

God You are so good to me. I was feeling discouraged and slow today then while eating my breakfast I gazed over at my books and read the title, "The Secret Diary of Elisabeth Leseur." It was one of the books that one of my yoga students gifted me. And though I've glanced at the title a million times today those words meant more. I grabbed it and blazed through Elisabeth's secrets. She bore the unbearable with a soft, humble grace *as her heart stayed locked on You.*

Her entries look similar to the way mine do on these pages. Some days we only write three sentences and on other days the stories stretch out to chapter lengths. *Thank You for my angels… **Your** angels. Thank You for Elisabeth Leseur's example today. I am spoiled by Your love. You are GOOD.*

I am edified today in this creative process. An inch of me was doubting my work here, but now I see **most definitely** these pages are purposed and worth completing.

Monday September 10th 2018,

Confession—there have been times where I have concluded that earth is hell.

Quickly, now my spirit is guided to the reality of the world, and the only Anchor who keeps my feet in the grass.

I do **understand** that life is not one long story of torture, but I don't always **know** this.

Help me.

Last night at Bridgetown the leaders called people down for prayer like they usually do. They called a couple of people down for specific things, **then** one of the pastors had a sense that someone named Melody needed prayer, and I knew that was a name I was to answer to. So, I went to the altar.

That's probably a name God would call me... I have the ability to come up with endless melodies.

I can't wait to share our songs.

My mind is the kind that reads so heavily between the lines that seldomly do I read the actual lines.

I was prayed for about music. Its makings must be blessed.

Tuesday September 11th 2018,

Yay! I think. Coffee Boy finally got my number... But within the first string of texts he's already used a kissy face. That's too forward. That's definitely a turn-off for me. **But,** when we were chatting at New Seasons he turned his head and I noticed he had a cross tattooed behind his ear... That's good news.

Right?

Now to wait as life unravels to see whether he's a participating (pursuing life with God) believer or not. That matters to me.

I cleansed my Instagram again. I deleted any pictures that portrayed me being or doing anything I don't want others to associate with me now. There were still a lot of pictures where I was dressed inappropriately or partying wildly...

Friday September 14th 2018,

Last night's meeting with Nick Emerson was **perfect.** Nick is Jami's older brother. She connected him and I because Nick is a record producer. We had a beer, and it was great great great to be nerds and talk about music. He's really passionate about it. His energy inspires me. I loved how he peeled back the layers and showed me some of his creation's births. He's going to show me his ways!

I'm ready to work.

Saturday September 15th 2018,

I will feel a freedom that matches each ray of light that is shone upon my life.

Sunday September 16th 2018,

I wouldn't call myself OCD, I would say that I have high perceptions. Like when you throw a pillow down, and your water glass is near... I recognize all the dust fluff's that could fly into the water, and I try not to cringe.

The last person I thought I had a connection with ended up being a **married** man with poor boundaries, so (monkey hands-to-face emoji)...

The bible is so fun to read. I love getting direction about whatever I am doing. Whether it's knowing what I'm free from, knowing where the sky gives no limits, or knowing where to go knowing, it's **good.**

Jesus, call me into cool things. For the rest of my days, I ask that You swoop in and let me create for work. Let's create the kind of artful structures that ooze life.

Am I doing enough justice? Do you see enough fruit off of my life like was spoken today at the Bridgetown Community Leadership Training? Which of the following could use some intentional God-Shayla evaluation time?

Love: does the fruit of love show in my life?

Joy: does the fruit of joy show in my life?

Peace: does the fruit of peace show in my life?

Patience: does the fruit of patience show in my life?

Kindness: does the fruit of kindness show in my life?

Goodness: does the fruit of goodness show in my life?

Gentleness: does the fruit of gentleness show in my life?

Self-Control: does the fruit of self-control show in my life?

I still have this: "liar-liar pants on fire" vibe about myself. When I step into church, no matter how much I "show up" I still feel less than worthy. I still feel less than righteous. It's probably because I know where I've been. I'm not yet mature enough to feel free from my sins like the bible says I am.

I have an exhausted mind. It's breathless. It's going-going-going, moving-moving-moving to the better me; the higher mountain, the wiser woman, and the steadier Shayla. There is a war of convictions in my mind. I have to put my hope in the reality that the top of the mountain will give me a better view of life. I anticipate a better quality of life with each drop of wisdom I squeeze into my mind. But I also need rest. I have an expectancy of His grace and direction.

God, I hear You when You say,

Be patient with Rocky.

(My sister's boyfriend's roommate, whom I met at my sister's birthday party.)

And I don't know exactly what this is about, but I will let my heart draw the best conclusion. The best for Your Kingdom is the best that could happen for anyone. So, I conclude: this means to be patient with this guy, pointing faithfully to You (this conclusion gave me a full breath of peace air).

I would love to integrate camping into my newly wedded life. I would love this. Somewhere new though, somewhere that's different than all my other times. Camping would be lovely for a first thing to do because it's tough to set up, travel and coordinate together. Could we have a tour bus or something similar?

Monday September 17th 2018,

As I sit here in this coffee shop, the barista is talking to a couple of older men about her enneagram type right now.

One thing I have noticed is that many need a box to function within.

For me, a box drives me nuts. This probably goes hand-in-hand with whatever box I test into.

Last night my subconscious was being **worked** in my nightmares; I tried to keep my eyes open so the dreams would stop, but I believe God allowed whomever it was to bother me so I could get to know the strength obtained from the simple whisper of song. During the terrors I tried to choke out, "You are not welcome here. In the name of Jesus, leave." And I tried to recite any scripture I could think of but the only fluent phrase I declared was: "Your ride this up on she shy."

Useless—to me at least.

Then I sang, "Turn your eyes upon Jesus," over and over until finally I slipped back into sleep.

There's got to be something so revealing about the quick subconscious-to-conscious responses we give.

Bluntly honest heart-blurtations.

Before the last of the four hugs Coffee Boy and I exchanged at New Seasons yesterday I said to him, "I'm not giving you another hug, that's just greedy." To which he quickly replied, "Oh, that's okay, I'll take everything I can get from you," while he reached for a final hug.

A quick dialogue in passing. I understand the non-concreteness of that interaction but the thought of having as much of me as he could was **obviously** on the brink of his mind... Bleh.

And I heard You when You said,

Don't pursue him while we were on the drive back from church yesterday. I asked You what You thought about Coffee Boy and then You responded.

For a while now I had boiled the statement down to: "Okay yes—I won't pursue him, I will let him pursue me."

But, in my love story I will only trust a man who shows up making me feel like the goodness I am through his actions and words. I love that Coffee Boy tells me that I'm beautiful, but I am patient for a man who is also dying to know how I will help him make the world a better place by pulling the kingdom down to earth as it is in heaven.

And anyways, life has unraveled quickly. Coffee Boy texted me saying that he wants to cuddle me.

I told him I don't give out cuddles so quickly.

Goodbye Coffee Boy.

Tuesday September 18th 2018,

Healing is my job title. It's hard. It feels like I dance to a different rhythm every day. Sometimes it's impossible to move to the beat. It's easier when I smoke weed and then come back to life rested so I can try again.

Dreams

God gave me a cool dream a while ago. In it I climbed a very high mountain with a lot of people. Everyone faded away until it was only my hiking partner and myself (he was in incredible shape). It was a strange trip that gave me a vulnerably empty feeling. I felt the work of the mountain on my body, it was hard. The climb was narrow at the top and through the final stretch my partner began fading into spirit. He was still **right there,** but gone. As we approached the top, I sensed another spirit on my right, stronger and **more** than this spirit on my left. We completed our journey and I rested on the high peak as a woman who appeared out of nowhere collapsed onto me and sobbed, her head on my chest. I brought her strength.

Interpretation

This dream is about the hard climb through healing I'm on with Jesus. It's about us working out and climbing together. It's about His spirit, the Holy Spirit, being with me even when I can't see Jesus. The third man is the final figure in the Holy Trinity, God. At the end of this journey instead of celebrating my hard work in solitude, I will be in shape enough to be strong for those who need me. I can't help but sense that this particular mountain is the mountain of healing from sexual abuse.

If this is the future You have for me, please bring me people who need to see the way You've healed me.

Thursday September 20th 2018,

Demons: I've never learned that they could materialize into this realm and hurt you (unless they possess a being). *But the bruise that looks like a grab mark on my thigh?*

I haven't even done anything yet today and already I need to meditate.

It's silly, the rhythm of life.

Weed... I was driving to go buy some because I wanted some. I have been nervous and having freak-outs recently (and caught in the cycle of turning to food to give myself love, and a substance to be filled with). It feels like I have stripped myself from all delightful indulgences, so I keep tweaking out and going on withdrawal-binges.

And a woman rear ended me on my way to the pot shop. She *barely* hit me but still, it's left me heavily weighing marijuana's existence in my life.

I had a massive headache lying in bed last night, which was new. I did feast on a heavy vegan-Nutella creation I whipped up, coconut butter, coconut oil, palm oil, honey, and cacao. Then I foolishly anticipated rest afterwards.

Two days ago, I was chatting with God (I wasn't listening **too** deep because I haven't been able to do that much lately). I was freaking out and sharing with him that I needed to do **more.** My dialogue went something like this: *"In the real-world people have jobs. They have traumatic things happen to them and then they have to continue functioning. They have to. But I haven't had to. I'm not working because You've provided me with plenty. Why have You blessed me so much? Not everyone gets the same grace I have received right now."*

Take my mom for example…

My dad's in jail and has thrown wrenches into our lives, yet she has had to work her usual, full load as an Accounts Payable Manager at a health insurance company here in Portland. She diligently shows up and does her best work. It's unbelievable that there isn't a pause button for when hell visits earth like it has in my family.

Like, timeout, satan just took a little bit more from me than is okay, I'll be back soon.

There is no pause button. Not for my mom. Not now.

Last night I called mom because I needed comfort. I was on the brink of a meltdown. It was caused by an accumulation of things, but the cherry-topper was that I scrolled through pictures on my phone to find a portrait of my whole family laughing together, about seven years ago. Then the whole, "How-could-he-do-what-he-did-when-he-acted-so-otherwise-at-all-times," doubt-train that makes it hard to believe the truth of the abuse took off behind my forehead.

Help me. Help my mom.

Friday September 21st 2018,

At our last meeting, before either of the grand jury's, we sat in The District Attorney's office. It looked and felt like a lawyer's office. He asked me what I "do." I explained to him, "I write about what you and I meet about. I first wrote [during the investigation] for my psychological health, then I started seeing the pages as pieces to a book because of the positive comments about my health while going through this process." He encouragingly nodded.

In faith I write.

In faith I write.

Monday September 24th 2018,

1:29AM.

It's time to jot down all the mind-riff's I've slapped onto sticky notes over the last month or so...

- My back hurts from heels, so I won't wear them. I think that's God guarding me from dressing up with attention-seeking desires.

- To create more time for Jesus, I will cut out DOUBT.

- If you edited a song as you produced it, you would save yourself time from having to listen to it over and over later.

- As a musician, I think it's okay to have the intention to spread your creation with no plan of performing.

Wednesday September 26th 2018,

It's 1:10AM. These last few days were amazing. I don't know where to begin so I am going to take the sequential route and see what happens.

I spent all of Sunday night hanging out with God, I didn't sleep. We wrote two new songs that I love. Monday morning was spirt-filled and relaxing: a 5AM bath, and later, yoga. Contemplations of whether or not it was okay to smoke marijuana danced through my mind. Then that afternoon rolled around, and I was feeling **good.** I had worked out, spent the day with God, and fed myself well. That evening I headed to Fear No Music (a show Nick invited me to) early because I wanted to walk around downtown and grab a beer. During the drive I was debating again about smoking marijuana later. On some days God flat out says,

Don't smoke today

and it evaporates the battle in my mind so I can save energy. But on this special Monday **I** concluded that **I just shouldn't smoke period.** It is not allowed on my condo's property—so I should not smoke because I don't want to do even one thing that would be disobeying God. He asks me to obey the authority He's placed over me.

115

"Let every person be subject to the governing authorities. For there is no authority except from God, and those that exist have been instituted by God. Therefore, whoever resists the authorities resists what God has appointed, and those who resist will incur judgment."

Romans 13:1-2 ESV

WHOA. "Whoever resists the authorities resists what God has appointed, and those who resist will incur judgement." My landlord has the authority over allowing certain things on the land I rent from him. He's not my governor or anything, but I have agreed to adhere to his rules for this place I live in. So, I definitely want out of incurring judgement. Goodbye marijuana. It might not be a forever goodbye, but that decision is for another day. A clear mind = heightened spiritual senses. I don't think I need marijuana to tolerate life anymore. I've used it to mellow out, check out, check in, ditch pain and reach for a band aid. And I just don't need it right now. And I know that after I smoke, I shouldn't drive. So, I definitely can't be of help to anyone who needs me to show up. And, conversations are harder to have because I didn't want anyone to ever know I'm stoned because I feel guilty about not being ready to help. I **do** however appreciate the rested ramifications of the after high.

Can I use it in a small enough dose so that I don't officially dissociate from life?

Can I save myself mind-time for other, better things than thinking about whether or not I should smoke?

Can I use it in a way that is not band-aid-slapping over my problems?

,

Back to Monday. I went and got my beer before Fear No Music and walked around for quite some time before the show. I rounded a corner to a church to walk by the front steps. There was a mob of young, clearly joy-filled religious adults.

"Is your name Rebecca?" One of the girls asked me.

"No." I said.

"Oh, I'm looking for a Rebecca to pray for her leg." She finished.

"My friend's leg is hurting." I told her truthfully, while I thought of Crystal Moore, a good friend and fierce woman for Christ. She's in crutches because of knee injuries. "You can pray for her."

"And let's pray for you!" She responded.

I was so down for this oozingly bright crowd to huddle around me. They asked me what I needed prayer for, and I said my back.

A few of them started praying at the same time for healing for me physically, then one of the women drew close to me and asked, "Are you a musician?"

"Well, I'm making music, yeah." I clarified.

"I see you on a stage, with a guitar, and God's saying, 'I want this more than you.'" She shared.

I was so blessed. So touched. I was lovingly assaulted by God outside of those church steps. He chose to encourage me further into this plan I'm working on.

Thursday September 27th 2018

It hasn't stopped, excited pacing while waiting for a friend to come over (I've done it since I was little). I'm twenty-three and I still don't know what to do with myself in the moments before a friend arrives. Alla Stasyuk (my friend from church) comes over this morning. I'm looking forward to showing her my place and getting to know her better! She's elegant, she's real, and she goes after things. She motivates me.

Friday September 28th 2018,

AH. You filled my spirit last night. While we prayed during community group, I felt angels over my shoulders.

It's truly so edifying to grow with a bunch of my brothers and sisters. I'm happy that Jan commented, "Because the hardest journey a believer will ever have to take is his own." Because YES sometimes I feel selfish living my own life and being stuck in it but hey: this is the story You've put me in. This is the life I'm living and I'm happy to go through trials with You. I sat at that dining room table with my brothers and sisters, confident of everything You've done in me. I am confident about the way You will move all of us to You. I ask You to help us confess wounds so we can dump your gold truth into them for each other. YOU ARE GOOD.

As the prayer time was closing, You rested two angels over me. I felt their warmth and Your words falling out of my mouth. I ask that You make our group rise together. Show all of the goods, uglies and amazing's of me that You want to. I know You've raised me to stand tall in your name so LET'S. Since I've volunteered to be the group leader, make me the leader each of them needs. Make me the sister each of them needs. I fall into Your trust.

I feel good about being our community group leader. When I told Jami that I volunteered myself for the position, she voted, "Nooo." She'd rather see people lead me through this season and not the other way around. I think that leading a group comes naturally to me, so, I'll do it.

Tuesday October 2nd 2018,

Can I tell you something funny?

Well, it's not funny per se but it's figuratively "off" when measured by the human mind.

I just received a call from an automated woman about a, "Last call to lower your credit card interest rates…" There have been a few numbers calling me like this, and somehow some of these calls have been asking for a Daniel (that's my dad's name) and immediately I am teleported from "lala-land" into hard reality. I wonder if they are looking for him and if somehow they got my number? Or, I wonder if it's a strange coincidence. Nonetheless here's the "funny" thing: sometimes I smell a "smell." It's metallic, and toxic-like. When I smell it, it triggers me to **get attentive** to the situation to see what I need to wise up to. Today when I smelt that smell when this number called me, I prayed that light would fall into this potential scammer's life and that any lies would be permanently demolished.

Sometimes this scent differs… But I know it's praying time when it wafts through the air.

Thursday October 4th 2018,

I saw Callum, my old boss from Krispy Kreme, driving yesterday for dominos. I've thought about him a few times lately so that was an interesting happening. Fun fact: I did not have a single donut while working at Krispy Kreme. I thought, "I don't want to have even one because if I have one, I'll have one every day, so no-thank-you."

119

I've enrolled in Institute of Integrative Nutrition's Holistic Health Coach Training program (so that I can learn more about nurturing myself with good food). It's very educational and diverse, we focus on the **whole health** of a being. (Mind, body, relationships, the environment we live in, etc.) It's causing me to discover deep intentions of mine, and to slow down and enjoy what I have.

The homework rocks, too. I like writing the summaries and doing the self-evaluations, they give me perspective and peace.

A Little Self-Evaluation Love from the Institute of Integrative Nutrition

"Who are you as a person right now in this current moment?"

I am a driven learner right now. I am energized to show up and soak up knowledge. I am basking in the rhythms of creativity.

"How do you show up in your life personally and professionally?"

Personally, I show up expecting to have to exert in a motherly way. This gives me anxiety when going to spend time with **anyone** who is a believer. I think of the facade required and am overwhelmed with what they're looking for in me.

Professionally, I show up with an overwhelmed feeling of what needs to be done.
1. I feel overwhelmed with how much more work I have to do in the books I'm writing.
2. I feel overwhelmed with how little I can put together with music. (I don't know how to do anything past

writing the lyrics and recording the melodies in my voice notes.)

3. I feel overwhelmed with how far off a finished demo seems to be. I want to finish an album!

I also show up with the duality of a hopeful heart. *God... I am sorry for not trusting You. I can't have both a trusting heart and an anxious heart. The space in me is big but it's not big enough to house the two.*

"What strengths do you see?"

I see wisdom as a strength. I have an aura of peace as a strength. There's a soft knowing about me. I am slow to fear or wither. I am quick to take all that is good and put it in my back pocket. I see and embody confidence in something that's past myself. You can see it in the way I move. I have found strength in something greater than myself.

"What weaknesses do you notice?"

I notice an addiction to food. I see a puffiness in my face that I could live without. I see an often-unkempt look about me that would benefit from consistent love and care...

"Who would you like to be peering back at you [in the mirror] in one year, five years?"

In one year, I would love to see a woman with steady compassion to gaze back at me. I would love to see a woman with a humbled demeanor because she's received God's **love.** In five years, I would love to be staring back at a woman who indefinitely calls others to marvel in His love.

"Ten years, and beyond?"

In ten years, I would love to gaze back at a woman, and a wife who reflects the eyes of God into any eyes that look into hers.

"If you could be your ideal future self, who would you choose to be on the inside and on the outside?"

I would choose to be a woman who reflects the eyes of God into any eyes who look my way. I would be a musician who in God-confidence declares utter truth over listeners. I would be a writer whose books spark fires in hearts that cause forward-healing action.

"How would you show up in your life personally and professionally if you were your ideal self?"

If I was my ideal self I would show up in my personal life with God-confidence. I'd rest in the Shayla He's created **to this date.** I'd be one who laughs quick, consoles gently and rejoices audaciously. My shoulders would rest lower and my stomach would feel more grounded.

If I was my ideal professional self I would show up with that same sense of God-confidence, exuding **trust, love, respect and responsibility**. I would declare more of the truth in my songs. I would fully embody notes and lyrics. In my writings I would be clearer with what I have noticed in my life.

"Notice if this exercise brought up feelings of insecurity or made you feel inspired about where you're headed..."[1]

This exercise makes me inspired about what I am working on AND HOW GOD IS WORKING ON IT IN ME. And I am reminded about how attainable the easy yoke of gifted

---

[1] The Institute of Integrative Nutrition® (IIN), New York City, founded in 1992. Quotations from the 2018 Health Coach Training Course.

blessedness on earth actually is. Not to say that this Jesus-walk isn't going to be tough, but the gifts are real! His provision is real! I believe He's blessed me with ideas around creating music. Music wasn't my plan. Even this morning I confessed to Him, *"This is so random."* But, it's **so inspired.** I can see how He will use this venture to work so much out of me so that I can be like Him in every way. *AH You are good.*

It's time for celebration! And a responsibility of commitment on my part. My hand is on the plow and I cannot turn around!

AS I KNOW BETTER, I WILL GROW TO BE BETTER.

Thank you to the woman who just walked by me at Barista. Your perfume is nostalgic to me. Kari… That's who it makes me think of. She was [is] a safe, calm, peaceful haven of a presence I loved to have around as a child. God bless you (Kari, and this stranger). Throughout life I am randomly comforted by this perfume. Its timely sweetness never fades.

Mmm, yummy yummy. Now a girl walked by with the same perfume Nichoal Dahrens (an old coworker that used to work at Black Rock Coffee Bar with me) used to wear. Yay! Nichol is **the best.** We grew to have a deep friendship, and her work ethic encouraged me to stay hardworking. She's a blast.

What lovely memories.

Uhg… A little bit of me just got hit with that, **"What is the reason for anything?"** feeling. Eavesdropping isn't my style but the men sitting next to me are chatting about God and one of them is specifically talking about his lack of church attendance and I'm thinking, *Well, if this random dude knows You, God, then perhaps all random dudes know You. So, what are we doing waiting for Your arrival?*

A tiny Frenchie (WHO ARE YOU) now strolls into my eyesight to make me cry thinking about adopting one into my life to **deal** with my puppy issues (long story).

Sunday October 7th 2018,

On the way to church this evening, You said,

Write me a story.

Okay.

A Story for God
Written by Shayla Danielle Laurendeau

There was a girl who was promised gifts so often that she started to doubt all the goodness set ahead of her. One day she had enough of this annoying doubt and decided that for one week she would believe every prophecy and beautiful promise spoken over her by her brothers, sisters, and the word. She found this one week to bring nothing but goodness, so she then committed one month of trusting every interesting thought she knew wasn't hers, nor a lie, and only good fruit grew. After this she then committed three months, and then the rest of her life to trusting her Creator's word for a blessed, functional, real, spiritually full life.

AMEN.

I have had a tough battle bursting through to believing the truth because of the lies that lived in my life. And **now** the man who raised me to turn to the bible, and to **get right** with God is opposing the truth I've confessed...

```
Deny, deny, deny. Lie, lie, lie.
```

He says, "This didn't happen." And I tried to tell that to the memories that came back. But they won't listen. They don't disappear. For 12 years they were gone. And now they're back. And they're real.

The good things that are happening in this world are too small. Let's do bigger.

What's up with being a prophet for your own life, is that a thing? 'Cause it is for me. Can I please have some prophecies for others? 'Cause this gift needs to be shared.

You are healing me from the inside out. Let me believe. I need to lay down and accept. You are good. Too good—and I am drawn Your way. Take my body. Take my mind. Let's dive over glitter.

I didn't take my hat off for five seconds today in church, You asked me to and I should have… I was ashamed because I was afraid of my hair being a little greasy.

You're making every bit of my body better. I thank You. Here we go.

Babe, I'll need you to listen through this next section.

Thank you to the man whose dream at the dream interpretation conference was **to go big with writing.** And how he said that God said it was,

Go big or go home.

YES. Thank you.

Prophecy

After the first blast of success from releasing creations of truth I will find a downfall. Only to then be met with a burst of wind to be more supplemental than the first successes could have ever absorbed. AMEN. *Your strength is made perfect in my weakness. I take You, in all.*

Tuesday October 9th 2018,

The movie Mountain Top is about to change my life. I know it. *Jesus, speak through this. God, have Your way in the way I interpret its meanings. Let me listen and sober up.*

```
Since when did I start spending so much
time reflecting on my wounds instead of
moving forward with the strength I've
gained because of the lessons they taught
me?
```

Thursday October 11th 2018,

Dream

I was sitting in a chair in a classroom like setting in a big supermarket. There were people all around me, we were at some sort of training. A few people were called on to share and they began thoroughly describing each of their ailments. The first one was a large woman I did not know. The second one to share was Cecilia Lame (a school friend of mine when I was younger). Finally, I interjected, saying, "When you go back with the physician you can tell him all the details." The class finished and we all started running around the supermarket. It was really, really huge. Mariah (another school friend and soccer teammate of mine) and I found a couple balls. One red, one blue. We started playing catch with Fernanda Manzano (also a school friend and soccer teammate

126

of mine). There was an important physician there. He was tall and walking around. He had a kid (not with him but for some reason I just knew this). I had a feeling he was interested in me. He jumped into our game and played with us. There were some other boys running around, interested in playing with us girls. I could feel the exciting air of potential-mates. The game had me really working. I kept catching the ball strangely, on my chest or in between two fingers, and sometimes dropping it. I then found myself on the ends of one of the isles writing in a notebook, I was in a brain-purge session where my writing was just expression. The physician hovered over my shoulder and read some of my notes out loud, "And their diagnoses prove them to be idioms." I was embarrassed, but I also didn't mind. I said, "Yes, I just write when my mind is twirling to get it out so I can flow in life more."

Interpretation

This dream is about the Bridgetown Apprentice Cohort. In it we'll have space to share our stories. It seems to be so that my patience and authority will be tested here, too. I told Cecilia that she, "can tell him all the details," because it seemed to me too much for her to share each ailment in that particular setting. The supermarket symbolizes what these people and I are filling ourselves with. In this case, it's good instruction. My school friends and old teammates symbolize the relationships that I'll experience in the Apprentice Cohort. You have to count on your teammates, and they're better at different things than you, and that's a gift. The red and blue balls truly make me think politically, about republicans and democrats. The fact that these women and I can play catch with political differences in our hands is beautiful. And the physician immediately makes me think of Jesus, He's the Great Physician.

To a man who was disabled for a long time,

"Jesus said to him, 'Stand up! Pick up your mat and walk.' Immediately the man was healed, and he picked up his mat and started walking. (Now that day was a Sabbath.)"

John 5:8-9 NET

There's no physician like savage Jesus.

In my dream I also had a feeling that he was romantically interested in me, so I do wonder if Jesus' likeness nods to the character of a potential future mate of mine. And because he had a child, I wonder if my future husband will have a child, or a life equally developed as if he did have a child. And since I was catching these political differences uniquely and sometimes dropping them, this nods to my humanness. Even while in a largely good environment I will fumble. I will "drop the ball." But that's what my teammates are for, practice and help. When the rest of the guys drew around and seemed to be interested in us girls, it draws the picture of life. The co-ed experience and supermarket of life.

I ate a whole jar of almond butter last night. *I am sorry…* I am untamed. I gave in to the long distraction of an eating session.

I feel really hot today. It's a weird sort of warm. Maybe it's my wool blend socks?

I am sitting here at Barista and **again** this little Frenchie has waddled in, cute and bringing joy into my life. *Are You prompting me?*

Preach

Last night, I finally realized that the Isaiah character that has been popping up in my dreams is God's way of telling me to study that book in the bible. So, I did.

There was a section where God described to Isaiah that:

"In that day seven women will take hold of one man and say, 'We will eat our own food and provide our own clothes; only let us be called by your name. Take away our disgrace!'"
Isaiah 4:1 NIV

In this passage God is revealing Jerusalem's future to Isaiah. I wonder when this will be. I wonder if that day is now. The day when women are desperate for men. The day when women are dying to get married so that their shame will evaporate. The shame of singleness. The shame of uselessness. Shame that's not from God. Shame is not from God. When we're feeling shame it's because the accuser (satan) is trying to make us feel bad for where we are. NO. GUILT is shame's sister, and our helper so that we don't do something wrong (lie, cheat, steal, covet, etc.). Guilt is a healthy emotion that instructs us to do the right thing so we can act righteously.

Anyways, when will Isaiah 4:1 be the present day?

I accept the pain in my body as thorns in my flesh, like the Apostle Paul did so he would not be conceited or haughty.

God is good. I'm good at the spiritual discipline of "silence and solitude." (Quietly waiting and listening before the Lord.) I was forced into it years ago. I broke my jaw after that bad car accident, and since it hurts to talk when your jaw is broken, I learned how to get really good at listening.

October 13th 2018,

129

Thank You Jesus that what I did for vanity helped my jaw stay safe and heal, XO. You have the power to make beauty from every vain (and pure) effort of mine.

Thursday October 18th 2018,

On the drive here (to the Bridgetown Apprentice Cohort) we spoke about work. We talked about how I feel like I should get a job after I get back from Australia... I told You that I don't feel like I am doing much. And, I told You that if I am called to "Sing," like You whisper so consistently over me... Then, I should work my booty off creating music. Music is a new territory... And, I needn't say much else than that. Lord, I trust you. **This** *I know: of all that I know, pursuing singing with You would refine me on my walk of becoming like You.*

HA. AH. You are gentle (as always to me). On Thursdays we fast [that means just black coffee and water until 7PM] *but this morning I forgot and made my full-on coffee. Coffee +* alternative *milk + honey + cinnamon and nutmeg.*

As I made the coffee my thoughts played ping pong.

- *"Well, then... What makes today different from any other day?"*

- *"Well (since it's fasting day) dinner is not until 7PM..."*

- *"Yes, so what makes today different from any other day?"*

And mindlessly through the coffee making I went.

But I didn't have honey...

*Then on the drive to cohort I tasted my coffee, and it was **bleh**. The almond milk and coffee had curdled. I tasted it again, and **bleh**. Then, I remembered my commitment to fast on Thursdays and how I accidentally broke it. So, it made all the weird coffee mishaps of the morning funnier.*

Ha-ha. It's moments like these when I am simply reminded that I walk with You. I make plans with You, and sometimes I fail to remember them, but You're always there to teach me and show me. You're right there in the plans too, and in my thoughts, directing me.

When I forgot about my plan to fast, maybe God allowed my coffee to get curdled just to tell me that He loves me and that when I fail to complete my plans, He's willing to step in.

"In their hearts humans plan their course, but the Lord establishes their steps." Proverbs 16:9 NIV

Thank You God, because sometimes we simply forget.

MAN, I miss my dad. I keep "seeing" him in other people in the world. I keep missing him. Sometimes I get revelations of God's character and then spiral into thinking about the Godlike characteristics that are in my dad. It would be helpful to work all of this out with a therapist... I want to see someone other than the two therapists I've seen. One of them is formulaic and the other seems shocked when I share with her the things my dad did to me. She's not new to counseling but she seems new to a story like mine. My story isn't new. It's not the first time a daddy has taken what he wasn't supposed to from his little girl.

On my walk after chatting with Crystal Moore I was reveling at all You're doing in her and will. The movement and purpose she lives with in her life?! Yes! I can't wait to see all that You and her will do.

Dang it—some thoughts hit me sideways
last night.

- "How do you feel about Rocky [Martin]?" (Kelsey's boyfriend's cute roommate.)

- "Well I feel indifferent really, he didn't reply to my last text, which doesn't matter because I understand I am to be patient and expectant of all good things. I feel like I am not to harbor a fantasy of what could be."

I loved chatting with Alla about her journey to her husband Slavic, it made me have peace about the fact that my love story is **not my duty** to manifest. She was minding her business and using her gifts to serve others, and then—**boom:** Slavic appeared. My future relationship **is,** like all things, an opportunity to grow in communion with God. It's a thing to pray about and hope for.

Thank you, pastor Gavin Bennet, for stating at Cohort, "As Christians we are not promised a life free of pain, but it's how we journey through this pain." You are right.

I cannot be, feel or act guilty for being a beautiful woman. AH. Shame be GONE. I dress myself in a modest nature so that I don't cause others to stumble. I show up and I live from boundaries that I am still trying to figure out. And that's okay. I am thankful for Mike, who is married to Ryn. I am thankful for Slavic Stasyuk, married to Alla. And I am thankful for Jan Weinstein, married to Sylvia. These men help me get used to men with healthy boundaries.

So… it's holiday season.

And this year my dad is in jail for sexually abusing me as a child. This makes me feel stale. This year things are getting better with my Kelsey, whereas they were stiff in years prior. We drifted because life does that to people. This year's closeness with her brings hope to me, even though things will never be so easily simple as they used to be when we were little, only fighting or not fighting over childish things. *And this year I have been living as hard as I can for You, Jesus.* That brings peace as warm as a blanket over me.

This year I want to celebrate differently. I don't want to hate the world through all of the upcoming holidays. This year I want to respond with celebration, like I am BLESSED to. This year I want to drink wine and play games with my girls.

This year for the holidays I want to dress how I like to be dressed. Probably with braided hair in three sections. Probably with mascara and a little bit of blush. Probably adorned in a few necklaces and earrings. Rings filling my right hand and my bralette for a bra, as per usual.

Honestly, I don't have people that are just "my people." I don't have people that I randomly go meet up with to do things… I don't have friendships that I'm really engaging in. My Christian friends from my old churches probably all think I'm a crazy party whacko—and at Bridgetown everyone lives too far to hang out with often. And in my other friend circles I honestly wonder if people think I'm a crazy lady. I've heard rumors of them thinking so.

God… Do I need to move closer to church so I can engage in friendships? What are we doing? What do I do?

OKAY JESUS, I SEE YOU.

I just met Traci. She was sitting across the table from me at Barista. We had a **soul hang.** She's a light. We started chatting and I told her, "I'm writing." And she said, "I had a feeling that you were writing." For some reason this made me feel really good. I ended up telling her what I was writing (The Healing Diary) and why I was writing it (to share how I seem to be doing fine during a time when it would be normal that I crumble).

Then we focused on her.

God, please help Traci.

Traci From North Carolina,

I am sorry that your family didn't believe you when you told that them you were sexually abused… And I am sorry that your dad disowned you and you were not in his will as a result of it…

F#ck,
Shayla Danielle Laurendeau

Wednesday October 24th 2018,

As I sit in my morning chair downing my coffee, I pray about my two worries today.

- *Whether or not You'd love me to start teaching two fitness classes at EDGE.*
- *And how I could go to visit dad.*

We did some soul work last night before bed as I massaged my stomach and the deep tissues of my psoas. With my eyes closed I wondered:

What would it look like to visit dad in jail?

I started to follow a vision... Several times my thoughts trailed elsewhere but then I saw my old bedroom. The scene of most crimes. I had a different view, Your view? You gave me scissors and together we cut up the whole dark scene... Then we peeled a filmy, rubbery casing off of the remains with a single left-handed gesture. On my bed, dad was wearing white, and I was wearing white... He was in a mix of tears and confessions explaining to me how his dad would come in the house and hurt them...

What was this?

Thursday October 25th 2018,

Sweet Barista at Black Rock Coffee Bar in Portland,

I write for you this morning. "To work in a coffee shop without working at a coffee shop, that's the dream." You said.

You're funny,
Shayla Danielle Laurendeau

I can't stop myself from singing along to the music overhead. *God keep pushing me this way! Keep pushing me into music. It is well. It is good. It is Your delight to hear me and for me to create for You. Rock with me my love! Rock with me and listen to my la-las with the <u>upmost</u> (New Girl reference) joy. I am seeing music more and more as a tool of communication and sanctification. This has to be Your intent.*

Note

Bethany Allen. *God, thank You for her. Watching her live her life in front of us while she pastors us in church and in the Apprentice Cohort gives me permission to live my story out how I know was made to. She's a lovely woman who's expressive and genuine, and energized by righteousness and*

You. Watching the way she goes after things encourages me to pursue the good things You've put in my heart. My name is Shayla Laurendeau and I have unique tastes and gifts that are specific to me.

On the Road to Music

In Response to Institute of Integrative Nutrition's Homework Questions

The Institute of Integrative Nutrition has unexpectedly encouraged me to go for what I was shy to admit before. I enrolled in the Holistic Health Coach Certification with the intention to teach people about nutrition after its completion. As the course progressed, I was slowly pushed to deal with my life and career fears. I had time to look at what I was doing and to see that I really could build whatever I wanted (Lord willing). When it came to work, I got honest about truly being in love (and gifted) with teaching. I like teaching about life. I like doing this through songs, and writing. I'm working on collaborating with editors, producers, guitarists, pianists and violinists, all for the benefit of my listeners' ears. I want to provide them with top-quality soul-songs that invite them into thoughts of, "La-la-la, am I doing the best I can? How can I be as free as Shayla says I can?"

Music is my top creative priority right now. That means I'm showing up to each session with Nick, applying as much energy as I can. Looking ahead at my ideal career, the aspects that really light me up are thinking about sharing creation moments with people as we cohesively spread the truth. And, getting to see lives around me gloriously heal because of truth delights me already.

As humans, we should be open to changing our course at times. Staying true to our word is an important virtue but finding the balance of seeing commitments through and jumping when it's time to jump is the sweet stuff. Yes, I **was** going to be a Health Coach but, Institute of Integrative

Nutrition's Holistic Health Coach Certification has empowered me to jump on the ship of my teaching (by ways of singing and writing) career, so—this is the new ship! I will still be coaching people, but through art.

Friday October 26th 2018,

You know what I've noticed? Guys are scared. They look terrified of women. How to act around them, what to say to them—all of it. It's like their faces whisper, "Do I open this door for her?" "Do I compliment her?" "Do I encourage her?" "She seems stronger than me." "She seems wiser than me."

*Last night I was praying to You and honestly, I am not sure what I asked. It was something along the lines of: "Guide me…" That's usually where my prayers go. I absolutely want to live life **for and with** You! And You gave me a vision of jewelry. Semi-fine jewelry at a booth. It was decorated in white… And it was similar to Noonday Collection's style. At least that's the name that came to my head… Maybe I am to do a jewelry line with them? Or sell jewelry at concerts? Or sell jewelry outright? Work in my heart…*

I am preparing to sing.
I am preparing to dance.
I am preparing to lead.
I am preparing to teach.
I am preparing for speeches.
I am preparing for motherhood.
I am preparing to speak truth,
I am preparing to exercise patience.
I am preparing to ROCK.
I am preparing to receive compliments.
I am preparing to stay in YOU.
I am preparing to publish short stories and my books.
I am preparing to LOVE.
I am preparing to guide.

I am preparing to live by example.
I am preparing to have "the hard" conversations.
I am preparing to trust fall into Your arms, daily.
I am preparing to live life with the fruit of the spirit on me.

You are TOO generous. Let me handle You better. You GIFT ME ALWAYS. YOU LOVE ME ALWAYS. YOU GIVE ME MORE. YOU GIVE ME BETTER. YOU ARE A PERFECT FATHER.

GOD, I have asked You to anoint my music, so that the ears who hear are split with Your spirit ringing truth. And I ask that you MOVE through this music. Make it a weapon against the enemy.

I am caring less and less about the stuff of this world. Fully desiring You is what my heart is beating for now. GIVE ME MORE OF THIS. LET ME HANDLE, APPRECIATE AND ADORE MORE OF YOU.

Monday October 29th 2018,

I remember when I was about 8, I would critique songs heavily. It fascinated me; the direction people took with words. Some were really weird, some were beautiful, and some I'd practice. I MISS this time. I miss having a CD and a CD player and being stuck with the same 10-18 songs. You had no choice but to **really** listen to them. A simple time.

From a young age, my teaching gift was attacked. I was silenced and got locked jaw due to injuries from my dad raping my mouth. I was quiet when he abused me. The nature of a human in danger is to cry out when we need to, but I wasn't allowed to. To this day I have a hard time saying what I need to so that I can be safe. I've stuffed cries down in my body and their memories still nibble on my bones.

138

"I want to try something," My dad said one night. He raped me anally and I whispered, "I don't like it, please stop." To which he said, "Shh." In his I-don't-want-to-hear-another-word-voice.

Years later I was hit head-on by a man who was driving drunk, and I was physically traumatized again. As a result of that accident my jaw broke and I hardly spoke for almost a year. Now I think that I'm obviously meant to say something to the world. Otherwise, what was all this opposition for?

Forever will I cherish this gift of a voice You've given me. Even if while on earth some force has success in silencing me, our words will be sung. The story You want to tell through my life will be screamed. You're holding me. I'm in love with You.

Tuesday November 1st 2018,

Anger wants to hang out with me today, but I don't want to hang out with him.

Right now, I'm researching Trauma Therapy & Counseling Services and reading about brain spotting; it's where a therapist guides your eyes to certain vantage points so you can access emotions and related brain functions... I'm wondering what would happen if I did this. *Would it help me process the unprocessed trauma that makes my body ill?*

I want to send a tattoo inquiry today.

I CAN'T BREATHE. I HAVE AN ITCH. AN ITCH FOR CHANGE. AN ITCH TO EXPERIENCE, AN ITCH TO MOVE. TO LOVE. TO BREATHE.

I FEEL LIKE I COULD CRY HAPPILY RIGHT NOW, just as I did last night after calling Tim Davis, telling him of the prophetic dream I had for him. That was a hard phone call because his pastoral leadership is authoritative to me, so I obviously don't want to be some crazy dream-lady who tells you what her magic crystal sleep cycle told her. But it was cool. He gave me wonderful guidance to consider when dreams like this are given to me.

I am meant for music... I never stop moving when it's on. *Lord, it's a lie that You won't give me wisdom when I need it. You are the curator of my heart... The director of my soul. And, that being said... How do You feel about yoga? There are many people who are worried about yoga being influenced by evil spirits. DAD, it's something I love to do for my body. It's a discipline I enjoy. It gives me great breathing-ability and strength. Give me Your nudges if there are evil spirits or any poison in practicing yoga.*

I have not been practicing yoga lately because I felt spiritual warfare around it. I would hear yeses and no's from the holy spirit (or spirit's) during my practice, and I was nervous to disobey God. And then my dear friend Jenna Orsini was praying for me, and she said that she sensed that God was leading me towards not doing yoga... So, after a few more reluctant practices, I've stopped.

But what I realize today is that I HURT. It's not normal to carry the physical pain that I do. I can be noble and say, *"Well, others have it worse, so I conquer on for them."* But Jesus says His purpose is to bring us life, and have it to the full.

"The thief comes only to steal and kill and destroy; **I have come that they may have life, and have it to the full."** John 10:10 NIV

It definitely feels like the thief is destroying my body and stealing peace. So, I'm looking to Jesus to help me have life to the full. For now, my pain is my fire. It's not my life. It's not my identity. I am not: Shayla Danielle Laurendeau, 200 Hour Registered Yoga Teacher and Pain Holder.

Sign me up to stare into the happenings of my life. The moments that have shaped me to be anything but an imago dei of You my King. Heal me.

Ahhh. The aching that rests over my body. Kill it. Let's move forward, even if it's trip-falling-face-down forward.

I truly want more friends. On this lonely island I find myself writing and singing away. Maybe this angst is the wind into next season.

Walk with me... Please. I don't feel well, I don't...

Thursday November 8th 2018,

I've emailed Noonday Collection regarding collaborating with them. *Lord this has to be You, encouraging me forward through creation. [You're in] Every. Little. Detail. You're making my mission more intricate than I could have dreamt with my heart, made with my hands or conceptualized in my mind. Take me into Your angelic type ways.*

I step to You. That's what the most recent tattoo we got is about. The X's on my knuckles are the marks to remind me to knock on doors. Your doors especially. Papa, I'm knocking. I am saying, "Introduce me to the people who are more excited than I am about the music I have been creating. Introduce me... Empower me to empower them to empower Your children." AH. Father. I accept. I accept more. Calm my spirit as I relay, speak and show up.

Prayers to You, Papa:

For the rest of my days would I die of pleasure if every day we rhythmically found time together.

And that's that. You've found time. You created it. So, to that AMEN. And to You I say, keep my heart only satisfied with You at the beginning of everything I prioritize.

I say gracias.

Papa, I don't deserve the aching's in my soul. I feel dirty. Wash me, forgive me. Thank You for this good day today. Thank You that I am here in Australia visiting Jami's new home. Thank You that You are so kind to me, telling me where to put my time and my heart. Enable my friends to hear what I say and to listen with discernment. AH. It's a rocking You've put inside of me. A little bit of rap mixed with some "heyyyyyaaa" melodies! I want to give You this gift. I don't know what the future of these songs will look like, but You've continued to say,

Wait. Wait for me to show you.

I am so encouraged by the way people describe my music style as, "unique." AH. *You keep giving little pushes and nudges daily, and I ask that while we are on this journey of climbing that I truly keep my heart tuned to You and to what You are doing in my brothers and sisters now and in the future. I pull and will not stop pulling inspiration from everything You're dancing around me. Thank You that You are truly my father. Just like the bible says,*

"A father to the fatherless, a defender of widows, is God in his holy dwelling." Psalm 68:5 NIV

I have a father here on earth, but he's not really fathering me. You have stepped in completely.

Tuesday November 13th 2018,

I guess I am just wondering why I am so gifted to know, to know, to know... *Why do You generously give me visions of what is to be?*

Is it because I listen to You and choose to?

Monday November 20th 2018,

I didn't know how to write much while I was in Australia. My days went in loops. Loops of: *"What do I do with this day?"* And, *"Isn't life supposed to go really smoothly and bless me right now?" But You had other plans. You had plans to show me what it looks like to live in this world as an engaged human. I spent my days journaling with You, going on walks, and meeting new people. I am so thankful I got to meet Jesmin, Jami's roommate, and their friends. They* **live** *in this world. Not in the way You say not to—but in an involved way that is* **good.** *So often I find myself living in another world (because I can, really). I can live all day in the spirit with You (praying, singing and writing). This fills me. But You have also created me to work, and to develop relationships, and to celebrate! Most of these things I am out of touch with.*

What are the practical human ways I can engage with life right now?

I can get singing lessons. I have the gift of singing, but I need to develop it. I can practice my guitar. This I know would be a wonderful tool in my singing and songwriting ventures. I can join the prayer team at Bridgetown. I am FULL because of all of the prayer I have received at church (perks of going down to the alter regularly). It's time to share what I've received! I can read the bible. I have found that this is the most effective tool for keeping me at peace, and my eyes looking at what God is doing, instead of spiraling through the inevitable troubles of life.

I am thankful for the unexpected things that I am encouraged to do because of my trip to Australia.

I went to Australia for two reasons; number one was to visit Jami, and number two was to go to the Hillsong Creative Conference. Jami and I both went to it. She goes to church there. The Creative Conference is an annual event they hold to inspire and equip people with confidence for their ventures. It's for people who have businesses, books, music, crafts, etc., that they're working on. They had a lot of different workshops we got to enroll in and attend. Prior to going, I had an expectation that I would make contacts at the conference that would propel my album into quicker or further completion, but again, God had other plans. As I sat through the workshops and heard the key speakers share about their creative ventures, I realized that I was already doing what each of them explained in their own way. Faithfully working on what is in front of them, and uniquely watching God swoop in with finishing touches, provision, and direction.

I was specifically encouraged by the founder of The Giving Keys, Caitlin Crosby. She was there to share her story. She used to be in the entertainment industry as an actress, singer and songwriter but she was also artistically finding ways to empower others. Through a couple of different inspirations, she happened upon putting encouraging sayings on old keys and making them into necklaces. She started selling them on tour and giving them to people who were going through hard times. She encouraged people to gift the necklaces forward once they were encouraged enough by the sayings. Caitlin said it wasn't long until the keys started outselling her album sales at her shows. And then, one day she saw a homeless couple on Hollywood Boulevard. She invited them to dinner and listened to their story. The woman mentioned that she made jewelry, and immediately Caitlin realized that she wanted to hire this couple to make the necklaces. The couple agreed, and now, literally, the rest is history. She has a successful business where she sells The Giving Keys and employs people going through tough situations and homelessness. She says none of this business was her plan. But God seemed to work out every effort of hers to bless her and so many others. AMEN.

While each speaker spoke, I realized that the simple pattern of their stories was: they went for things and God made something out of their work. They did not have everything planned out, nor did they have all the money, but God made a way.

On one of the conference nights, Jami and the girls we carpooled with were ready to go home but I still had rehearsal for the choir I was in to perform "I'm Getting Ready" with Tasha Cobbs Leonard on the final night. I told Jami I was okay with finding a ride home because I didn't want to miss practice.

I worked the whole night at finding a ride home. I connected with people in the alto and soprano sections but came up with nothing. No one was headed towards Jami's. I started to panic a bit. People fizzled out and I was almost sold on ordering an expensive taxi but then someone told Shekeinah Hill that I was about to pay a load for my ride home, so she insisted on driving me instead. She works at Hillsong. She coordinates a lot of the music performances there. Jami's house was about 40 minutes the opposite direction from Shekeinah's, I was blown away by her generosity.

Thank you for loving me, Shekeinah.

And whoa, dude. Tasha is one of those singers who *sangs* in rehearsals. It was royally impressive.

Thursday November 22nd 2018,

Thanksgiving.

As I sit here at 11:17PM I thank You for guiding me through the rivers of life. You have me constantly climbing out of boxes. In Australia You made it clear that you want me to develop the non-Christian songs that we have written. I wanted to go the Christian-musician route (because I thought it'd be easier), I thought I'd be a fun shock-value [with my tattoos, piercings and yoga teaching background]. But You've told me to la-la my way into the world's music for now, not Christian music.

My sound will not be the beep-boppy stuff that's out there. No way. Thank You for giving me gentle, private rebuke-like nudges to get my butt into gear.

When I was in Australia, I walked a long way to a park. The trail covered me in sweet smelling jasmine flower, as did most of the parks in Australia that I wandered through. This park had a football field and people running on trails for their morning workouts. I walked to the top of the highest hill and sat on a bench while I watched the buildings downtown. Then I pulled out my diary because I wanted to talk to God about music.

Ten songs.
Is what God said to me.

Ten songs.
He repeated.

I knew He meant that we were about to choose ten songs to focus on. Perhaps the ten songs that would be on my album.

As we scrolled through my phone it felt obvious to me to choose the worship songs I had been writing. But something didn't feel right about that.

No worship ones.

He said.

Slowly but surely, we chose more than ten and I really fought for some because I thought they were good, but He made it clear that those were not songs for this album.

Shayla, I don't want you singing Christian music on a Christian album for your first album.

I was overwhelmed. To me that actually made sense. I have stories I want to sing to both believers and non-believers.

First, **Dancer** was listed. It's a song about strippers, and how they might feel fulfilled while they're dancing in the chaos of the music, but how there is an open invitation for them to "Come home," away from pressure and heartache, into Jesus' arms.

Wild was next. This song is about what I think earth will be like after the second coming, after God renews it.

Then we had **Flower**, that song is about the fact that my father took my virginity.

Rapunzel is about staying abstinent and being patient to wait for a good man. It's a song about working on your dreams and using the creative energy you long to. It's about the fact that while a woman is waiting for a man to come into her life, she has time to bless the world with the gifts she has.

Gas Mask is about the infectious joy that I have, and that if you don't want it, you'll need your gas mask, 'cause it's contagious.

Human Love is about warming up to the idea of falling in love.

Rhythmic Cadence is about maliciously beautiful women. It's about being careful not to be one, and about being careful not to fall for one.

Holy Night is about the night that I remembered that my dad abused me. It's about how a single prayer shattered earth so that heaven could come down over me.

H20 is about being incredibly thirsty for God's love. It's about my struggle to feel satisfied with it.

Hues is about racism. It's about the pressure and divisiveness the devil desires for the world.

Tuesday November 27th 2018,

Where are You? You say that I will fall into Your peace, and that I get Your peace as I stay in You. All I have done is gone a little off course. I'm counting on You to swoop in with Your supernatural abilities, I've thrown my efforts out the window.

I don't want to give up. My true heart (the deepest part of me) says, "No, we will not give up! We are a voice, and a being of love, and of reason."

Where are You? Promiser of peace? Where are You when I slip down the mountain and am unable to use my strength to find anything to cling to? Where are You when I cannot feel anything? Where are You when I can feel everything and it's all pain? Every bone's end is scraping the next. These pinching acute levels of agony cause my character to break when I can't take it anymore.

The silence through the pain.

I feel the heavyweight of Your request for me to live.

I truly feel like a cracked-out nonsense girl at church. I feel like I'm broken and look frazzled.

I am in pain. Head to toe. I ignore it because it's fallen way behind on the list of heart space important things. I wonder why my physical ache seems to scream louder than my heart's aches.

Free me. If freedom is Your word for me, I want it. Freedom. Help me.

John Mark Comer taught us about our "flesh" and sinful nature on Sunday. He talked about our cravings and used Ephesians 2:3 as a reference. It reads,

"All of us also lived among them at one time, gratifying the cravings of our flesh and following its desires and thoughts. Like the rest, we were by nature deserving of wrath." Ephesians 2:3 NIV

Paul wrote this to show that he too very well knew about living to satisfy his desires and following his cravings. John Mark showed us that in another book Paul brings this topic up again by saying,

"For when we were in the flesh, the sinful passions which were aroused by the law were at work in our members to bear fruit to death." Romans 7:5 NKJV

149

Here Paul is describing that while he and other believers lived to satisfy their desires, it caused them death, or in other words, a toxicity or inability to give and bear life. He's sharing that the satiation of our devious passions (i.e., wanting to have an affair with a married person, sex before marriage, stealing so we can have what we want, cheating to get ahead) lead to spiritual death. "The law" Paul mentions in Romans 7:5 is the set of commandments we are to abide by. He says that he found that the law itself provoked sinful passions that led to sin. Probably because with rules set before you, it's common to want what's not allowed, unless you're free from satisfying your fleshy passions. Unless you understand the goodness that comes from denying yourself. I dare you to figure out why it would be good to say no to yourself, and yes to God.

"The heart wants what it wants." - That's a quote from a man who married his adopted oldest daughter.

Wednesday November 28th 2018,

You are so kind to me... After battling through the should-I's around accepting the yoga position offered to me, we went on a walk and finally I sensed You say that I shouldn't.

Man... Honesty: I don't feel good. My body hurts...

In the evenings You insert goodness into my subconscious for it to bubble up and out during conscious times. I exalt You. Thank You. Creative book ideas have bubbled up. I love You, King.

Thursday November 29th 2018,

2:29AM.

To get to the end of yourself, to the brink of your capacity, that is the goal. That's the place where I see God lean back and say, "Now let me show you what I do." When I slam my wounded places shut, I can block God from creating a radiance through my pain. When there are too many doors shut on the walk of discovering what it's like to live like Jesus, a human can burst. Down goes the creature, slipping off life's cliff after maximum efforts, screaming at its Creator, "Help! You say You will! You promise You have plans not to harm me! You promise fruition after my efforts! WHERE ARE YOU?" While all along The Creator is quietly working in every detail, reshaping the cliff so that its creation doesn't slip too far.

SO – during moments of silence and solitude/meditation there has been a thought (or prompt) that has been popping up in my head for months.

The prompt has been to call a boy (well, he's a man now) that I went to elementary school with and went "too far" with.

Today the thought came to me **again,** so I grabbed my phone. I had no plan, and I had no idea what I was going to say to him.

I dialed his number only to hear, "This number has been disconnected..."

And now I am wondering several things about this thought/prompt's happenings.

1. I wonder if the intention was for me to have a reconciliation conversation with this man.

2. But since his number has been disconnected… I wonder if the lesson was: not to hesitate when given prompts that I believe are from The Holy Spirit.

3. OR was my lesson the fact that: God will protect me when I think I'm following Him. He'll swoop in and

block me just to remind me that I am His child, He is my Father, He is the King of this world, and the phone lines.

Lord, You are so good to me. You see it all. When I am blind or shutting my eyes You say, "Just follow me." Like a walk through a haunted house, I close my eyes, scrunch up my shoulders and say, "Okay."

Monday December 3rd 2018,

I stalled writing over the weekend. I can almost not capacitate the goodness.

I ask for an increase, now of my abilities. I need to be able to hold the gifts You've showered me with. I want to foster them well. You are My Creator... My Everything... My Soul Song. My Love.

Wow. Where do I start? **Here:** in the middle of the swirling's of my mind. I'm going to number my thoughts so I can keep them straightish.

1. WELL, it's no coincidence that my car's lease is up in June. The Apprentice Cohort ends in June. **And** the bonus course with the Institute of Integrative Nutrition: *Launch Your Dream Book Course* ends in June.

2. Friday... Friday was the best of days. In the evening I had quite a bit of energy left in my tank at 6:30PM, so I texted Emily Johnson (best friend). The woman that loves me and has loved me through messes. I love her. "Are you working tonight?" I asked. She soon responded with, "No! Nick and I are going to a concert this evening! You should come! It's 'Zion I.'" YES, I agreed. I was shopping at that moment, so the drive home was filled with Zion I's music. I tried to buy tickets online when I got home, but it said

they were sold out. Something was shifting in the atmosphere, though… I **knew** I had to go. So, I got ready in faith. I wondered if Zion I was my dude, the artist I was looking for to jump on my song, "Dancer."

Go, but let's go at my pace tonight... God said. *Will you listen to my promptings? Will you trust my words?*

Yesses flooded out of my heart as I peacefully continued getting ready even after the show's start time. I daydreamed of bringing "Dancer," (which I was remastering while getting ready) to the guys backstage after expressing my collaboration interests to whomever I needed to in order to get to this guy so our creations could take flight. I charged my headphones and everything, I was fully prepared. My outfit rocked too. I wore my huge pink fluffy coat.

The drive to Star Theater was flooded with Zion I's music—and my prayers. Prayers for favor, prayers for direction, prayers for FUN, and prayers for wisdom. The more I listened to his music the more I wondered what God was up to… I didn't understand what was going on. But I stuck with the direction I sensed. My body was wrapped in excitement.

I got to the theater and chatted with the bouncer, Joe, about whether or not he liked the music, "Yeah, he's a good artist. A good man, too." He said, while he told me that he had known him for a while. That made me excited.

I got inside and the ticket dude exclaimed, "There you are! I have been waaaaiting for you to show up!" My soul appreciated his random, wild welcome as I continued to dwell in the presence of The Most High.

Now reflecting on this welcome I sense that that is the nature of Your welcome to me in this scene. Stepping out, showing up! AH.

Now in the venue, it was time for a beer... Then my memory zinged me with a fact from earlier: **before I even knew about the concert** I was at Target and I was craving an organic vegan peanut butter cup. I couldn't find one, so I thought maybe I'd find one at the next store. As I walked into the next shop's entrance, I heard the Lord say,

Skip the chocolate, let's get a beer tonight.

"Okay..." I thought. I wasn't really craving a beer, nor did any of the beer I had in my fridge sound good... Nor did going to McMenamins for their yummy ruby sound right... But I kept the pressing in my pocket and skipped the chocolate (only, honestly, because I couldn't find any at the second shop either).

And back to the concert. I met Rich Hunter on Friday night. He played before Zion I. Rich Hunter's beautiful soul sound would blend very well with my music. I got Rich's contact info and he said that he is open to chatting about making music together. God had a perfect plan.

Thursday December 6th 2018,

It's a good day when you're at a coffee shop and you watch a beautiful woman grab the attention of another woman just to tell her, "You're really beautiful," Then walk out.

Josh Porter... Thank you for teaching us about prayer at cohort this morning. You are a wise dude.

Josh sets different subjects to be the purposes of his prayers each day of the week. Whether he has things like family, coworkers, healing or restoration he was praying for, something different is set for each day. I wonder how much a rhythm like that could make you see more of God in your life. What happens if you pray persistently for God in different areas, areas other than only the ones that are stressing you out?

What do you see?

I see... Us standing in a still tornado of purple.

What does it feel like?

Ecstasy. Not the synthetic kind, but a divine kind that nurtures you. The kind that energizes you. It feels like I want to leave - but only to tell people about it. Or—I want to pull people in, and I'm not afraid about not being able to get back in.

How is this that we got here, Shayla?

Time... Trust... Encouragement. Your word. Prayer. Deliverance. Good people. Believing. Living by Your word.

What do you see, Shayla?

I see us staying in the still, deep purple tornado. I see us welcoming all who have ears [heart ears/soul ears].

What do you see, Shayla?

I see You changing the color now. It's blue. A light, bright, clear, Australian ocean blue. It's thin, and not complex. Simple. It's here washing over everything. Is this Your word, Creator?

Shayla, you are my word. It is good. It is well. You are good. Talk to me, Shiakana.

I've never heard that name before. A brief google search just taught me that in Hebrew Shiakana [Shakiana] means, "God's presence and glory." How peaceful and honored I am to have You name me as Your presence and glory. With You it's both and.

Father... I want to see Your redemption imparted in every being You've fearfully and wonderfully made.

I will honor that.

Where are my steps to You, today, father?

Stay in the fire. Notice who shows up today. Breathe...

I love You.

I am Your created being. I am the word from Your lips.

The vision of blue washing over the inside of the softly swirling purple tornado is me. I am a purifier (blue's symbolism) moving within the royal (purple's symbolism) tornado.

I.e., I am commissioned to purify those in the body of Christ (the royal priesthood).

Thank You for this deep and gentle loving on me today, Dad.

I am BLESSED to have begun voice lessons yesterday. My teacher Francine, is a **doll**. I feel comfortable with her and sense a sweet, sweet friendship brewing. PLUS, I'm an alto. I'm pumped. And YAY—we are going to use the songs I've written for practice!

Life, simply put, is just time on earth before eternity with Our Creator.

Friday December 7th 2018,

The most humbling technology thing just happened… I accidentally held down the control button and this whole book zipped into an email that almost emailed a lot of Bridgetown staff… What in the world?

God, I feel great today. Coffee with the lovely and wildly wise Kendra Yamin just wrapped up, and I feel great. I feel fabulous. I admire Kendra's pace. She doesn't move or speak in a rush. She's bold and an unmoving rock of a believer. She knows how You love and she's fierce to describe it to anyone who needs to hear. Let her influence all whom she needs to.

Saturday December 8th 2018,

Fire
A Poem by Shayla Laurendeau

"Fire."

Fire has found its way into my heart.

Fire is in the same heart that holds the ice I use to cool my wounds.

Fire is moving me from here to my purpose.

Fire is welcome.

Sunday December 9th 2018,

Can I be real? (I will be real, this is my book.) Things aren't **that** bad.

Even with everything about my dad. His situation doesn't feel like much of my problem. I am sad, of course. I'm sad that he's denying that he ever abused me, and that he's living in a jail cell right now… But my sadness is over there, in the Jesus box. To quote my friend Jan Weinstein, "Their sin is just not my problem." AH. There is so much freedom in that statement. It's not my fault that my dad is in jail. I did not tell that man to act illegally. That was his choice. It's with sadness that my family has journeyed through these burdens of sexual abuse and manipulation, but it's with freedom that I've casted those burdens on my savior.

Because of the shame I've felt, I've wanted to hide from my story. I wanted to hide behind a different name on Instagram, this book, music streaming platforms, and even Facebook. I wanted to start all over. I wanted to hide behind a different name because I was (am) afraid of what people (especially the ones who know me) would think once I confess the truth.

But you know what?

I have a name, and it's Shayla Danielle Laurendeau.

My name is my name not just for me, but for others to relate to me. My name is attached to my life's story. I want to bless others with what they see from my name. I want people to see all that God wants to show them though my name.

God. You've got to swoop in. Free me from my compulsion to eat whole bags of cookies. When it comes to sugar it's an all-or-nothing thing with me. Some people around me think it's funny, but it's toxic. It's an addiction. One I nurture every time I make the choice to make a sugar purchase. Food is a rough topic for me. I'm done typing about it.

My honest thoughts on the #metoo movement? Well... I've hid from social media because this hashtag is harvesting a reckoning inside of my soul.

```
Why would I want to put that hashtag up?
Why would I want more people look at me
with "Poor, wounded you," eyes? BLEH.
```

Thursday December 13th 2018,

Ah... The Apprentice Cohort was so great this morning.

We talked about imaginative prayer.

I feel more and more invited to play in places that I thought were no-no's... My church recognizes that God created us as imaginative beings. We're encouraged to pray and pay

159

attention to things that God might inspire us with, like pictures, feelings, or sayings. I have experienced these kinds of happenings in my prayers since I can remember, but I had never heard about it in church until now. Since going to Bridgetown I have been paying attention to what God stirs in me while I pray, instead of me only trying to find words to say or things to pray about.

Until now I wasn't sure certain qualities of mine belonged in the church.

BUT. God. He's that good. He's always got more to give.

Friday December 14th 2018,

I had a good time at the dentist yesterday. I always do. Everyone at my dentist's office is lovely. Dental appointments are prime soul-conversation times. I'm in my element in that chair. And I'm thankful I have a cavity.

I haven't been treating my body well. Sugar, I've been eating loads of it. That's why I am happy to have a cavity, because I am saying goodbye to sugar. And I don't think anything other than a cavity was going to stop me.

In that clinic chair I asked my dentist to take out the metal retainer bar that he put behind my bottom teeth. I told him it was because I believed that God wanted to heal my jaw more, but it needed to come out first.

He was overall amused, and complied.

The bar was supposed to be there permanently to keep my teeth from moving. But God's spoke to me about wanting to heal my jaw more, and that He needed the glory, not my dentist. The bar was put in some years after the car accident in 2015. After the initial hit, I spat pieces of my teeth out because my jaw had clamped down crookedly and some of them chipped. I was rushed to the hospital (LOOK AT GOD: **an ambulance happened to be two cars behind the accident).** In the imaging tests they found no evidence of my jaw being broken, nor was it causing me any issues. The only broken extremity was my right wrist. But in the months to come my jaw started sliding around, locking up, swelling up, and causing me pain that came to the end of unbearable. During that time, I saw my doctors more than I saw my family. I spoke in limited ways and could engage with others only a little because any expression was painful. In the past few years, I've wondered about the real culprit, was it the accident or the abuse that had its way with my jaw? I've wondered if the trauma from the accident stirred up wounds that I was deeply dissociated from. I've wondered who wounded my spine, my father, a car accident, or was it a compound effect? I've wondered where my inability to breathe properly comes from, being robbed and helpless in my innocence, or being insecure in the present?

For continued healing I need no answer. I need no culprit to pin my pain on. I don't need a scapegoat or a perpetrator to blame. I've done what I can to stand up for myself now. My invitation today is to give Jesus the case and let him fight for me, heal me, and love me.

Sunday December 16th 2018,

I have another document that I have been seldomly writing my "Wish-I-would-have-said's," in. It's not because I regret the past (although, **for sure,** sometimes), but because I want to practice getting clearer in the future. There are usually several "Wish-I-would-have-said's" in a day. The trick is to not let shame take over my body while recounting. My purpose for doing this is because I want every word of mine to build and bless. I don't want to fall into the droning buzz of the world. I want my words to be purpose-filled.

My jaw not being perfectly healed is an opportunity for You to grow my faith higher than the mountains. To: "sing," we go.

Monday December 17th 2018,

I am jazzed to continue healing. My new counselor, Laura, is great. I like how sensible she is. She's gifted in the literal-realm and I am gifted in the dreamy-realm, so having her counsel me will be great.

When receiving counsel, I want to practice more humility. I'd like to humbly accept guidance and correction.

AH. I'm in love with You. What is this vision of bright puzzle pieces You gave me last night?

You showed me chains, beads and bracelets on child's wrists, and I want to know what You're showing me...

"Truly I tell you, unless you change and become like little children, you will never enter the kingdom of heaven. Therefore, whoever takes the lowly position of this child is the greatest in the kingdom of heaven." Matthew 18:3-4 NLT

Wednesday December 19th 2018,

It's been a great day so far. I have been passionately breezing through the book, "The Practice of the Presence of God." There is something so gentle about the way it's writer, Brother Lawrence, lived for Our Creator. He simply used every moment to draw God into his mind. He imagined the presence of God around him as frequently as he could. I highly recommend this book. After the very short read, I trust that any reader could receive some of the peace that Brother Lawrence had. His walk with the Lord was built on a simple practice. No rules. Just work. Just acts of love. He said that every time he strayed from thinking about God for too long that God nudged him with reminders so that they would stay so sweetly close.

Today I am reminded of the truth of the bible. *I am reminded that the fruits of Your spirit or lack thereof are a direct depiction of where our allegiances lie.*

The Holy Spirit woke me last night. Two things were chanted into me. The first of which was,

Keep knocking

([keep trying] to make music). And The second was about a bus.

Envision life on a bus.

Okay! I got **really** excited, assuming that this was a tour bus for the life of a musician. Eeek. I can only pray, Lord willing. LORD WILL WHAT YOU WILL WITH ME.

"Diamond Lens," is a great name for the child sexual abuse screening service I'd like to create. I would love for it to be named, "God's Lens," but I think "Diamond Lens," has a more accepted ring to it. Oooh, what if we were able to get into schools across America?

I imagined testifying about the things my dad did to me last night. As I sat on the witness stand, I was asked, "Why is there an incessant smile across your face?" I replied with a larger smile, explaining that the closeness I have with Our Creator makes it to be so so that I cannot help but feel free.

We're going to court soon.

Thank You for my voice teacher, Francine. She is a gift. She's a kind, spirited reflection of You. You've purposely gifted me with a teacher who follows You. She is wonderful. Fear is falling off of my bones as I sing and learn how to do so properly. AMEN to all that You are doing. And another AMEN to whatever else we add to our rhythms. Help me say "No," when I need to next week so I can get a little more done. You've blessed me with friends and the kind of jobs [writing and music making] that I can do in between WHATEVER, and I want to dance in that for as long as You're commissioning me to. AMEN to doing life Your way. You are my gift. I breathe You in. AH. So much more You have to give me. I ask that I step in congruence with You always.

The clarity with which I am writing with right now surpasses delight. While I fast, You bring freedom through rest. I am typing in sync with the present moment. Usually, I am recounting something that has happened or processing something that I need to spit out, but today I am typing with the present. It feels good, **so** *good to be this empty. To be not ahead of myself nor behind. The rhythm You've pulled me into with Sabbath and fasting and sitting in Your presence has Your peace drowning me. I am down to forever stay stuck under these rumbling waves of grace. What a radical/dope life You give. Uhm. Now I'm a little speechless. And wow, doesn't this feel good.*

Forever... I seek to stay here with You. I actually feel like I am in another state of being. True. Empty. Ready. Believing. Delighted.

Before I crawled out of bed this morning, I asked You what You wanted my head set on today. You said,

Get up, do your things... We will be there.

And I said, "Great, that's dandy but I'm sure You have something You'd like to bring my way." And You said,

Blue, first thing, and dance with me.

Blue is our way of saying, "Read the word." And to: "Dance with me," I say: thank You for asking me to. I had under fifteen minutes until I needed to head to my voice lesson, and I was feeling down, in a funk (this fast has been harder than other times). But our dancing perked me up! And it was hard. We've been practicing with Latin music, which I can dance to well, but I'm more of a florally-noodle type mover so it's been challenging to tighten up my shapes.

You are so delicate with me... You flood my dreams with the next day's writings, and more.

Thursday December 20th 2018,

I'm sitting at Black Rock Coffee Bar in Portland (close to where cohort meets), and I'm drinking some lovely coffee, sitting in a lovely chair. There's a funny bit between my friend Savannah Charlish and me. We say its telepathy—but the fact is, is that I actually have no idea what she's thinking when she thinks I do. It's just that we give each other these all-knowing looks. "Telepals," that's what we've named ourselves.

Amen to all the goodness of being in sync with You. Amen to writing on my iPhone right now. It feels like the hardest spiritual discipline I've endured (I'd rather have myself a laptop that reads my head telepathically [like Savannah apparently does] but it's only 2018 and I would never allow technology in my head like that).

165

I'm happy we're here. At Black Rock. I was going to grab a cup of coffee at Barista, which would have been great. But being in this chair with my shoe off as my left leg is crossed underneath my body? Yes.

I have the gift of God's provision. He has no intention of ceasing His goodness to me. It's true. It's exactly what's in the bible and I choose to believe Him. I choose to trust every word He says. This means in His way and in my heart, I will gain His riches.

Does this mean I'll see Him provide for me financially next year like He did last year?

Does this mean my character traits will be richly endowed by the fruits of His spirit?

There's no verse that promises me that I will get the results I'm going after, but there is a verse in the bible that tells me that I will reap good if I sow good.

"Let him who is taught the word share in all good things with him who teaches. Do not be deceived. God is not mocked; for whatever a man sows, that he will also reap. For he who sows to his flesh will of the flesh reap corruption, but he who sows to the Spirit will of the Spirit reap everlasting life. And let us not grow weary while doing good, for in due season we shall reap if we do not lose heart. Therefore, as we have opportunity, let us do good to all, especially to those who are of the household of faith." Galatians 6:6-10.

And, since we've hopped on the truth-train here's another zinger from Jesus, "Truly I tell you, whoever believes in me will also do the works that I am doing. He will do even greater things than these, because I am going to the father." John 14:12.

DO YOU KNOW WHAT THIS MEANS? I have the ability to raise people from the dead. I have the ability to come back from the dead (I might need help from an earth-believer to ask Jesus for this but it's REAL). I can restore eyesight to the blind. I can move mountains. I can save all abused children. I can lead a country. I can sing professionally and successfully, each song unlocking evil binds that sat over beings, simultaneously replacing those binds with blessings. I can sing professionally even with jaw issues. I can teach creations about the eternal life that is GOD'S GIFT to us to receive. All of these things I can ask God for.

His will be done, above all else.

Thank you to the kind checker in Market of Choice that complimented my singing. *AMEN to YOU speaking through random encounters. AMEN to the fact that I cannot stop singing so I found myself indulging even while she rang up this morning's food.*

Friday December 21st 2018,

There is enough Holy Spirit juice in the body of Christ at Bridgetown Church so that an empty or broken soul can join the congregation in worship and praise on Sunday and be filled enough to conquer life until next week's gathering.

Saturday December 22nd,

You know, I felt **guilty** for not doing much work today. However, the work I have been doing is **so much,** and I have been pumping it out at a rate faster and **more** than I think I realize.

I am not depleted, but full. I am peaceful and whole. I have a feeling that I am almost done writing in this diary, even though the reason I began writing in it is hardly settled. I foresee nothing being able to blow this peace away. My Lord is with me, dwelling all around me, heavily.

AND WHAT A WIN today to not folding and eating sugar. Yay! I was craving it so badly. I can't handle having it in my diet right now. I don't have the self-control enough not to eat it all day if I indulge even once.

Heal me.

I need Your help in the media world. What's the thing in the media world that we should engage in right now?

For now, I believe it's posting videos on YouTube.

Monday December 24th 2018,

My heart aches today. It's not because of pain or sadness, but to do the work my soul sings for.

*Lord, permit me **by Your grace** to sing for Your nations.*

In Your kindness, Most Highness, You show up in my dreams to instruct me. The trick is to let go of all presumptions of what I think You might be saying so that You can speak fully through it's interpretation. It's best when I share my dreams with my wise friends. The ones who know Your dream language. Then, with their help Your perfect direction is made clear.

Wednesday December 26th 2018,

I could write about the good time that mom, Kelsey and I had yesterday for Christmas.

I could describe the many laughs that suffocated our chests.

I could tell you about the beginning of our new memories.

Or—I could say, I hope that your Christmas was at least as good as mine.

In January, my mother, my sister and I are scheduled to go to court. It's the state against my dad.

After I remembered that my dad abused me, I told Jami.

Then we told our pastor.

Then I told my sister Kelsey.

And shortly after I called a family meeting. My dad was sitting in one recliner, my mom was in the other. Kelsey was on the floor, near the sliding glass door.

I looked straight at my dad and said, "Dad, I remember what you did to me when I was little." His blank face showed that he was going to pretended that he didn't know what I was talking about. "That you molested me." I clarified. He laughed, denying ever doing anything like that. Then a feeling like I have never had before washed over my whole body. I spat out, "You're lying."

I had never felt such fire-like purity in my veins. It was like the spirit of truth took over me. A coolness took over under my skin while a warmth radiated out of me. He continued to deny, repeating over and over, "This didn't happen." While I countered, "You're lying." And now, since he will not confess, he's been in jail for a while and we're going to court.

My heart doesn't need to know what that will be like, or how it will end.

I do hold a true sadness inside for the state of my dad's being, and for the burden that our family is walking through. This sadness though, is coupled with the Divine's angelic legion medicating every ache.

This story is not over, *but the permanent trust I have in You is sealed.*

The promises about what will be created with the rest of my family's days have me needing not to record my innermost swirls anymore.

"And my God will supply every need of yours according to his riches in glory in Christ Jesus." Philippians 4:19 ESV

"Fear not, for I am with you; be not dismayed, for I am your God; I will strengthen you, I will help you, I will uphold you with my righteous right hand." Isaiah 41:10 NKJV

"For God so loved the world, that he gave his only Son, that whoever believes in him should not perish but have eternal life." John 3:16 ESV

"Do not be anxious about anything, but in everything by prayer and supplication with thanksgiving let your requests be made known to God. And the peace of God, which surpasses all understanding, will guard your hearts and your minds in Christ Jesus. Finally, brothers, whatever is true, whatever is honorable, whatever is just, whatever is pure, whatever is lovely, whatever is commendable, if there is any excellence, if there is anything worthy of praise, think about these things. What you have learned and received and heard and seen in me—practice these things, and the God of peace will be with you." Philippians 4:6-9 ESV

November 14th 2019,

On the morning that we went to court, I went to my regular Thursday morning commitment at Apprentice Cohort.

Showing up brought me a bit of normalcy on that irregular day. I rushed to court after the cohort. I hated that I was running late. There were no parking spots close to the courthouse, so when I found one I had to run several blocks in my wedges.

After the security check I asked for slightly panicked directions to the courtroom. Down the stairs I flew. Everyone who came was waiting for me at the bottom. I could tell they liked how I looked. In dark blue TOMs wedges, a nice top, navy pinstripe pants and a matching blazer, I did feel beautiful. I was fasting too, sort of unintentionally. How could I eat? My outfit looked gorgeous, and my insides felt the same.

Our team huddled up with us Laurendeau women and we ran through how the day was going to go. It sounded easy enough. Our Victim's Advocate warned us that dad might come in in a wheelchair because that could grant him more sympathy with the judge.

Lots of people were there for us, it was incredible. Tim Davis was there. Jeremy Bucher and Steve and Kristi Emerson (all friends from Christ the King Community Church in Canby, Oregon) were there. Lori, Janae, Dawn, Mari Petros, and Chuck and Debbie (all friends from the Oregon City Church of the Nazarene) were there. Alysa Ahrens and Jennifer (old family roommates and friends were there). My sister's boyfriend, Connor Davis, came to support us. Crystal Moore (my yoga-student turned soul-friend) came and on rare occasion was decked out in jewelry that she had to hilariously strip herself of on her way through security. It brightened the day a bit. Jenna Orsini and Savannah Charlish (close friends of mine from Bridgetown) were there.

There was a wild energy in the whole mass of us. We filled the end of the hallway with laughter. There were jokes and catching ups. I introduced my beautiful friends to one another. You could feel the presence of the Lord around us. I felt free.

And then it was almost time for the hearing to commence. The Victim's Advocate whispered to my mom, Kelsey and me that they were about to bring my dad through.

They rolled him down the hallway.

The crowd with us silently and audibly gasped.

He looked sicker than I've ever seen him look.

Ash was his skin tone.

Jail stripes covered his bones.

My body melted.

He didn't look at us. With his poor eyesight I don't know if he could have recognized even one of us family or "friends." He was slumped. I hated seeing him like that my whole life, with his shoulders sunken in, it was like he was holding his heart all by himself.

At this point I didn't feel bad for him. I saw the reality of what his actions had done. He caused so many people to have to support the Laurendeau women, so on that day I had very little pity. This court case was the result of his destructive choices. Us girls huddled into a holy little haven, and I said some wild stuff about there being angels around us.

His attorney… She looked like the lady-version of my dad. She looked terrified of me.

You could feel the atmosphere all day. It was like the presence of many believers called the Spirit of the Lord to the courtroom.

"For where two or three gather in my name, there I am with them." Matthew 18:20 NIV

I thank the Lord that my dad waived his right to a jury. To have even more people hear about the intimately painful circumstances would have made me sick. I was already naked enough having so many friends there.

It was time. I felt like I was walking into the job that God had been preparing me for for years. I was ready. Then they called my name to the stand. As a child of God, and a daughter to my dad, I had many things going through my mind while I walked to that witness stand. I thought, "My dad's going to be so proud of how healthy and beautiful I look right now." And, I feel bad for him, that we're here." And finally, "Wow. All of these people are here to support me, and my family." After those thoughts I was only a quarter of the way to the stand, so I spun around and leaned down to tell my dad, "I don't hate you." I said it softly enough so that it'd be between the two of us. His lawyer freaked out and so did the District Attorney. I had thought that talking to him probably wasn't allowed, that's why I didn't ask if I could.

Then it was as if I had laser-like focus and fierceness. The only other time I had remembered feeling so powerfully brave was the day that we had the family meeting. Both of these times I felt like a vessel for God. It was like He was using me and showing me my ability at the same time. It was terrifying and perfect.

The District Attorney asked me questions first. He was kind to caution me of the hard parts of each next step. He told me things would feel cold in the courtroom, and they did. He was the person my case got to. He's one of the ones who fought for me. For the law. He's the one the truth got to after the Lord caused me to remember.

I believe that the night I prayed in my mirror for God to deal with anything He needed to in my life, He nodded in agreement. The truth came out from hiding, and that's a good thing, so that was from God.

"Every good gift and every perfect gift is from above, and comes down from the Father of lights, with whom there is no variation or shadow of turning." James 1:17 NKJV

Truth is good.

It frees you.

After the night that the memories came back, I spent a few days writhing and praying over what settled back into my accessible memory. And then I called Jami. My stomach turned as we made plans to meet so I could tell her what was going on. I hoped I was crazy. I hoped that I had had some sort of mental break and that these memories could be explained away and discovered to be illusions. But that's not what happened. I met Jami at a big, beautiful house she was housesitting at, and I told her about the memories that came back.

She comforted me and shared with me that the same thing happened to a friend of hers recently. That gave me peace that I wasn't crazy. The memories were real. And even though they were dark, I couldn't shake the free feeling I had once they made their way through my body.

"And you will know the truth, and the truth will set you free." John 8:32 NLT

Jami and I met with our Pastor on that same day. He's no stranger to dealing with these sorts of happenings. He counseled me through what to do. I told Kelsey, and then we had the family meeting.

Kelsey reminded me recently that I called her down to my room because I was in wretched emotional pain a few days before I told her that I had remembered what dad did. I had asked her to pray for me. I told her I couldn't tell her what was going on, but that I needed her to pray. She said, in the unsaid that she thought that dad had molested me, and I was dealing with it. The thought popped into her mind before I ever told her. She said it was like the Holy Spirit was preparing her for what I was going to share.

Wow.

After the family meeting, on a summer day, I called the police. I couldn't go on without contacting another authority to handle the situation. Our pastor had already intervened, and through his and the church's counsel, my dad still didn't confess. I hadn't planned on getting the cops involved but my dad continued to lie and treat me oddly after I told him that I remembered what he did to me. He looked me in the eyes with sharp lies.

Darkness
A Poem by Shayla Danielle Laurendeau

I love you, baby.
He said to me multiple times in my last few days at the house.

Can I have a hug?
He asked.

"No." I replied, feeling empty.

My body racked with unrest, I quickly moved out. After time, counsel, and prayer, I dialed 911. I paced in Emily's backyard. I divulged a long, choppy, difficult confession about what my dad did to me. The deputy sounded young. It was shameful explaining my dad's acts. I felt bad that I gave deeply intimate details away. Then after some time, the Detective contacted me. I met with him a couple times as the investigation went on, and eventually they had enough cause to arrest my dad, so they did. I didn't have peace on the day they arrested him. I imagined my dad in a cement room, and I was scared. I learned that people in jail don't like people who have done what my dad has. I was scared for his life. He was already so frail and ill. And since then, sadness has stayed in my bones while I am also charged with purpose to conquer through life.

Then we met the District Attorney for the grand juries because we weren't done. My dad still hadn't confessed, and there wasn't enough evidence to convict him completely. It was his word vs. mine and our family's. During my testimony I made sure that the whole room knew that I had forgiven him. I made sure that the whole room knew that the only reason we were in that courtroom was because my dad refused to confess. The District Attorney's questions breezed by; they were tough to respond to. And then my dad's attorney was next.

She had evil in her and has lied for many people's sins, I could tell. And I was getting fidgety, how I do. I usually sit crossed-legged and lean on things and what not and I had been up there for quite some time now, so I leaned forward on the stand and propped my head up with my fists. (My friends later told me this melted their hearts with cuteness.) This lady could ask me questions all day. I was ready. Then some funny stuff happened. The District Attorney told me before court commenced that we could not mention the lie detector test in court. For some reason lie detector tests/results are inadmissible for use in court.

My dad's attorney asked me an encrypting question I couldn't decode. She asked me when and why the second detective was put on the case, and I was stuck. The second detective was put on the case to help with the lie detector test. I had sworn to tell the truth but was told that I couldn't bring up the test. I thought the moment was weird because dad's attorney was musing like she was about to hit a homerun. I treaded slowly, "Ever since the lie detector test that my da——." "YOUR HONOR." She exclaimed, defeated. Whatever her plan was didn't happen. She continued, "I had requested that that not be brought up in the courtroom." I apologized, saying that I thought that that was what she was asking about. The District Attorney cleared the air, declaring that he had informed me that I wasn't supposed to mention it. Time continued and more questions were asked and answered.

Then we got a break. I was congratulated by many, as if I had given a successful presidential candidate speech. My mom testified next. Then my sister. It was painful watching my mom reply to the lawyers' questions. She just wanted a life where she loved God, her husband, her children, and did best by them. But with those things came turmoil.

My mom told me that when we had the family meeting, before I told dad what I remembered, a still, small voice told her, "He molested her."

The Holy Spirit prepared my mom and my sister. He wanted the truth to be known.

It felt worse watching Kelsey on the stand. It's not like she signed up for these happenings either. She told the truth, that she didn't grow up having an estranged relationship with our dad. I thank God for protecting her. Then we were out of time, so we had to commence the following day. It sounded exhausting and exciting at the same time, having to go again.

The energy I was filled with was unreal, I still hadn't eaten, and it was almost dinner time. We made our way out, and on the steps in front of the courthouse, Jeremy Bucher thanked me for the grace he got to witness me give my dad. I was overwhelmed with gratitude for the way God was using me to show Christlikeness.

I had a music session with Nick planned that evening and I decided that my dad **would not** continue to steal from me, so I showed up. I was brain-dead and ate dried dates and laid on the floor. Nick told me he wasn't charging me for the day as he boomed loud orchestral music through the studio. I went home and slept okay, which was nice.

My dad testified on the second day (this surprised everyone, because he wasn't required to). He exaggerated in his favor and at one point seemed to explain that he had Alzheimer's, saying that sometimes his thoughts leave him. Whatever. I have never heard him talk about us girls as sweetly as he did on that stand. It was disgusting.

At one point while he was testifying the Lord said to me,

Shayla, I need you to get up and walk out right now.

It felt so strange, like I was making a scene... I obeyed, even though I wasn't sure if I was allowed to leave the courtroom.

The Victim's Advocate followed me out to check on me. I told her what God had said. She nodded, saying, "We've got to follow those things." Then we prayed.

My friends didn't tell me what my dad said after I left the courtroom, but they did say that he said something that he's said that's tortured me before. So, in that moment—in front of all those people, God wanted to spare me from feeling extra weight on that already heavy day.

Both detectives testified as well. You could tell that they were made for that kind of thing. My dad's attorney asked The Detective the same question she tried to trick me with, "When and why was the second detective put on the case?" He answered, abiding by the rules. He knew that he couldn't mention the lie detector test. He said, "Sometimes in cases of this matter a second detective is brought on to help." I think my dad's attorney was trying to undermine his abilities, making him look like a detective who couldn't do the job by himself, but I thought this was weird because I had already blurted out the truth about why the second detective was put on the case.

Everyone working on my side of the case (including my mom and sister) believed that this abuse happened, but my mom and sister's testimonies weakly supported mine. Neither of them had the same abusive experience with my dad that I did. Fast forward, and the verdict was about to come through. I sat right across from the judge. I was scared. This was the worst part. I had no idea what to do with my body. As she began relaying the ruling, I watched officers come into the courtroom and close in on my dad. Then she looked straight at me and said, "I believe you have these memories; I just believe they are false memories."

An empty shock washed over the courtroom. It seemed to be so that justice wasn't served.

I was thankful that she said that. Thank the Lord she motioned him as not guilty. I thought time would stay still for forever, and that my bones were going to implode and shatter inside of me while I saw those officers closing in to (again) arrest my father. My heart didn't want to see justice served on that day.

Like a teenage boy my father looked at his attorney, pleased. Everyone who came to support my family and me quickly dispersed out of the courtroom. I wanted to talk to the judge, but whatever. Our team and everyone who came with us shuffled across the street to a meeting room next to the DA's office to debrief. The District Attorney was composed and beside himself at the same time. He spoke brief, encouraging words, so did our Victim's Advocate. She asked if we all wanted to pray, and we did. We bowed our heads and held hands around what looked like one of the largest Thanksgiving tables I have ever seen. When she said amen, I chided in, saying, "Wait!" I couldn't get a song out of my head while my dad was testifying so I sang it there. I asked everyone to keep their eyes closed while I sang "Surrounded (Fight My Battles)." It's a triumphant song about the fact that it might look like you're losing, but really, you're surrounded by God. Some people started singing along. It was lovely.

There were tender "thank you-s" and heartbreaks expressed. Love rained on my family and me. I burst into tears then drew away to be alone. I paced the streets of downtown Oregon City and wrote a song. It's called "Final Judge." Maybe I'll show it to the world someday. It's about how God is the final judge. I never needed an earthly judge to rule the truth for me. That wasn't what I was after. I knew my job was to fight as far as I could for the truth, no matter the outcome. And frankly, I'm pleased my dad didn't go to jail again. I love him, and I forgive him. Even though he never apologized.

Made in United States
Orlando, FL
22 April 2022

17078945R10114